# ADVANCED**JAZZ**
# **GUITAR**CONCEPTS

Modern Jazz Guitar Soloing with Triad Pairs, Quartal Arpeggios, Exotic Scales & More...

## JENS**LARSEN**

FUNDAMENTAL**CHANGES**

# Advanced Jazz Guitar Concepts

**Modern Jazz Guitar Soloing with Triad Pairs, Quartal Arpeggios, Exotic Scales & More...**

ISBN: 978-1-78933-086-1

Published by **www.fundamental-changes.com**

Copyright © 2019 Jens Larsen

The moral right of this author has been asserted.

**www.fundamental-changes.com**

Twitter: @guitar_joseph

Over 10,000 fans on Facebook: **FundamentalChangesInGuitar**

Instagram: **FundamentalChanges**

For over 350 Free Guitar Lessons with Videos Check Out

**www.fundamental-changes.com**

Cover Image Copyright: Shutterstock: Miguel G. Saavedra

# Contents

# Free Scale Practice Lesson

Many of the examples in this book are derived from scale exercises. As a thank you for purchasing the book you can download a free video lesson, with advice and suggestions for practising the exercises. Get it by visiting this page on my website:

**https://jenslarsen.nl/freevideolesson/**

Bear in mind that due to the size of the video, it's best to download to a computer rather than a tablet / phone.

**For over 300 Free Guitar Lessons with Videos Check out:**

**www.jenslarsen.nl**

**Join 1000 other Jazz Guitarists on Facebook:**

**http://bit.ly/InsidersFBGroup**

# How to Use This Book

The second book in my Modern Jazz Guitar Concepts series focuses on cutting edge concepts that I don't see covered in other educational resources. These are the concepts I hear in the playing of musicians like Kurt Rosenwinkel, Chris Potter, Mike Moreno and Peter Bernstein, to name a few.

This book includes a set of standalone lessons you can use as a resource when practising a concept or working on a particular chord sequence. But I hope it will also provide you with a fresh perspective on modern jazz that will give your playing an injection of inspiration and creativity.

Each chapter begins with basic scale exercises and a short theoretical overview. This is followed by ten musical examples over the common II V I chord sequence that show different ways to make each concept musical while improvising. Together, the exercises and examples will embed the sound of each concept in your ears and help you understand how to put it to use in your playing.

All the examples in a chapter will be in the same key. I vary the key from chapter to chapter to offer material in most of the common jazz keys. Staying in the same key as you work through a chapter will help you to better understand what's going on – but once you are comfortable with the concepts and licks, you should absolutely practise the ideas in all keys.

While you can happily begin at Chapter One and work sequentially through this book, you might benefit from diving into certain chapters if you are looking for inspiration and something new to practise. You can even just pick out examples that resonate with you and use that as the starting point to study the concepts behind the licks. In my experience, jazz musicians don't learn things in a linear fashion and I'd argue that it's healthy to be led by your inspiration when choosing what to work on. That's definitely how I've learned best through the years.

## How to Study a Chapter in this Book

The overall aim is to assimilate the ideas in this book to the point where they become part of *your* vocabulary. It's easy to practise an exercise or learn a few licks, then move on – but this won't help you to internalise the music. Other people's licks can be also be unwieldy and don't always immediately fit into your playing. To this end, here is my advice on how to approach each chapter (using Chapter Two as an example):

Chapter Two discusses the concept of *triad pairs*. You'll learn what they are, how to find them for any chord, and examples of how to use them.

Once you have checked out the examples, begin to incorporate them into your playing. The most efficient way to do this is to work on two things:

1.  Write your own lines using triad pairs and explore how to make melodic lines that fit well with the other concepts used in your playing.

2.  Improvise freely using triad pairs over chord changes. Focus on using the lines and connections you built in the previous step.

It's important to play new ideas over familiar tunes and chord progressions – please do this, so that you can concentrate on the ideas themselves and not chasing the changes. But don't be tempted to bypass step one – do compose your own melodic lines, so that you are turning information into *real music* and, more importantly, *your music*.

## Composition as Practice for Improvisation

If you are familiar with my YouTube videos, you'll know that I spend a lot of time composing melodic lines to see how many variations can be achieved from one concept, and that I do this while playing *rubato* (freely, without a strict tempo).

I recommend this as a method of working with new concepts. Be a composer first, then an improviser. It will help you to develop very strong melodic lines. Edit out the ideas you don't like and focus on the ones you do – then develop them to your taste. Having the understanding and confidence to play music that is to your taste is a fundamental part of developing your identity as a unique, interesting musician.

Finally, though it is always a worthwhile exercise to understand the theory behind melodic lines and the notes that are used, don't forget to look at how the melodies are constructed. Understanding how melodic phrases work is almost a lost art in modern jazz. Be aware of melodic ideas like call and response and repeating motifs, and keep the big picture in mind: we want to create compelling musical ideas.

Learn jazz – make music!

*Jens*

# Get the Audio

The audio files for this book are available to download for free from **www.fundamental-changes.com.** The link is in the top right-hand corner. Simply select this book title from the drop-down menu and follow the instructions to get the audio.

We recommend that you download the files directly to your computer, not to your tablet, and extract them there before adding them to your media library. You can then put them on your tablet, iPod or burn them to CD. On the download page there is a help PDF and we also provide technical support via the contact form.

**For over 350 Free Guitar Lessons with Videos Check out:**

**www.fundamental-changes.com**

Twitter: **@guitar_joseph**

Over 10,000 fans on Facebook: **FundamentalChangesInGuitar**

Instagram: **FundamentalChanges**

# Chapter One: Tritone Substitution

A great way to generate new ideas for your solos is to find new ways to apply concepts you already know. In jazz, there is one re-harmonisation concept that has been around since swing and bebop eras that will allow us to do just that: the *tritone substitution*.

In this chapter we will explore what a tritone substitution is and how it works.

Example 1a shows a familiar II V I sequence in the key of G Major:

Am7 (II) – D7 (V) – Gmaj7 (I)

…followed by the same sequence with the tritone (or flat five) substitution applied:

Am7 (II) – Ab7 (bV) – Gmaj7 (I)

Most readers will probably be familiar with the sound of this substitution, but how does this new Ab7 chord work? To understand this, here is a short explanation of guide tones:

It is the 3rd and 7th intervals in a chord that define its quality:

- A chord with a major 3rd and major 7th = a major 7 chord

- A chord with a minor (flattened) 3rd and a minor (flattened) 7th = a minor 7 chord


These guide tones tell us what sort of chord we are dealing with. Similarly, a dominant 7 chord will always contain a major 3rd and a minor 7th (flattened seventh or b7 for short).

Here is the fun bit! A dominant chord always shares its guide tones with one other dominant chord that is *three tones* (AKA a tritone) away from the original chord. In music, this distance of three tones is referred to as a flattened fifth or b5 for short.

In our example, the dominant V chord (D7) contains the following notes:

F# (the 3rd)

C (the b7)


The chord a tritone (b5) above D7 is Ab7. This is what the interval looks like on the fretboard:

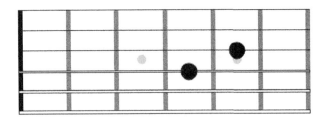

If we look at the guide tones of Ab7 we see that they are:

C (the 3rd)

Gb (the b7)

Gb is the same note as F#. In other words, Ab7 contains exactly the same guide tones as D7, but they are reversed. Since they are the strongest notes defining the chords, it means they are completely interchangeable. You can *always* substitute one dominant chord with another that is a b5 (tritone) away.

A bonus of applying this substitution to the II V I progression is that it creates a descending bassline that moves chromatically from Am7 to Gmaj7.

**Example 1a: II V I and II sub[V] I**

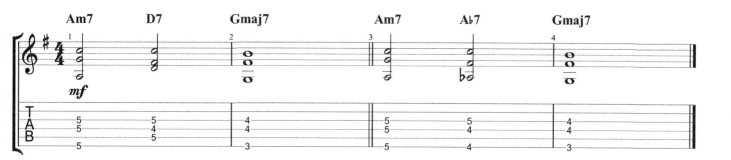

## Scale Choices for the Tritone Substitution

When confronted with a tritone substitution in a piece of music, what are the options for improvising over it? There are two logical scale options to play over Ab7 in this instance: Ab7 Mixolydian and Ab7 Lydian Dominant. The table below shows the notes for each scale:

| Ab Mixolydian | Ab | Bb | C | Db | Eb | F | Gb |
|---|---|---|---|---|---|---|---|
| Ab Lydian Dominant | Ab | Bb | C | D | Eb | F | Gb |

The formulas for the scales are:

Mixolydian: 1 2 3 4 5 6 b7

Lydian Dominant: 1 2 3 #4 5 6 b7

Notice that the only difference between these two scales is the fourth degree. The Lydian Dominant scale has a #4 (D). The Mixolydian has a Db and can therefore create a tension that sounds the furthest "out" from the key centre of G Major, especially against a D7 chord.

**Side note:** *Ab Lydian Dominant has the same notes as the D Altered scale – a common choice for playing over D7 if you want to create tension and resolution.*

The table below highlights the interesting, rich-sounding tensions that Ab Mixolydian creates when played over Ab7 and D7 chords respectively.

| Notes of Ab Mixolydian | Interval formed over Ab7 | Interval formed over D7 |
|---|---|---|
| Ab | 1 | b5 |
| Bb | 9 | b13 |
| C | 3 | b7 |
| Db | 4 | Maj7 |
| Eb | 5 | b9 |
| F | 13 | #9 |
| Gb / F# | b7 | 3 |

Notice the intervals that the scale draws out. Playing Ab Mixolydian over Ab7 will emphasise the 9th and 13th intervals. Played over D7, the same scale will create #9 and b13 intervals. These are powerful altered notes that create rich tensions, which can be resolved when the chord sequence moves back to Gmaj7.

## Useful Exercises to Check Out

Now we will look at some exercises designed to help you apply these ideas to the II V I progression. The following examples all use the tritone substitution in the chord progression, so the sequence is: Am7 – Ab7 – Gmaj7.

The aim of the exercises is to help you apply the Ab Mixolydian scale over the dominant chord and resolve your lines to Gmaj7, but first I want us to consider two other tools that are at our disposal.

First, in jazz it is common to create II V movements in any sequence, even if those chords are not there to begin with. For instance, if a dominant 7 chord is written in the music, it's common for jazz musicians to precede it with its II chord. In our II V I sequence, we can imagine that the Ab7 is preceded by its II chord (Ebm7) and play melodic material from that Ebm7 chord over the Ab7, increasing our melodic options.

Second, if you have read my previous book, *Modern Jazz Guitar Concepts*, you'll know that it's common to create material for jazz soloing by first learning a scale, then using the arpeggios that exist *within* it to create jazzy lines. The arpeggios that are formed on the root, 3rd, 5th and 7th of the scale are normally the best starting points for exploration.

Example 1b shows the Ab Mixolydian scale. For reasons of space, I only show one position of the scale. Do most of your practice here to begin with. Your main goal is to get the sound of the scale in your ears without worrying about other possible fingerings. Once you are extremely confident with the language you can create in this position, by all means explore it in all positions.

**Example 1b – Ab Mixolydian scale**

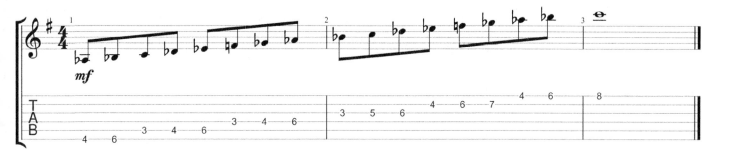

The following exercises (examples 1c to 1e) are designed to teach you how to connect the Am7, Ab7 and Gmaj7 chords in a meaningful, musical way. Remember, even though we are playing Ab7, the audience is *hearing* D7.

I've mentioned that the best diatonic arpeggios to use to create jazz lines are those based on the root, 3rd, 5th and 7th degrees of a scale. The table below spells out these arpeggios, drawn from the Ab Mixolydian scale.

| Root | Ab7 | Ab | C | Eb | Gb | | | |
|------|------|-----|---|-----|-----|-----|-----|---|
| 3 | Cm7b5 | | C | Eb | Gb | Bb | | |
| 5 | Ebm7 | | | Eb | Gb | Bb | Db | |
| b7 | Gbmaj7 | | | | Gb | Bb | Db | F |

Example 1c takes 7th arpeggios through short versions of the tritone II V I sequence. The chords remain the same throughout, but the arpeggios move up in diatonic thirds to include more extensions. The sequence of arpeggios is spelled out in the following table:

| Basic chords | Am7 | Ab7 | GMaj7 |
|--------------|-----|-----|-------|
| 1st Arpeggio set | Am7 | Ab7 | Gmaj7 |
| 2nd Arpeggio set | CMaj7 | Cm7b5 | Gmaj7 second inversion |
| 3rd Arpeggio set | Em7 | Ebm7 | Bm7 first inversion |

## Example 1c

*Am7, Ab7, Gmaj7 arpeggios*

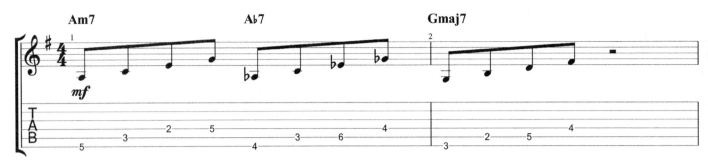

*Cmaj7, Cm7b5, Gmaj7 arpeggios*

*Em7, Ebm7, Bm7 arpeggios*

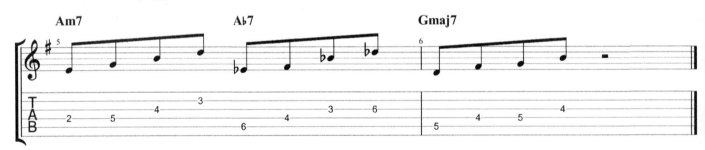

The useful *triads* built on the 1, 3, 5 and b7 intervals of Ab Mixolydian are illustrated below:

| Ab | Ab | C | Eb | | | |
|---|---|---|---|---|---|---|
| Cdim | | C | Eb | Gb | | |
| Ebm | | | Eb | Gb | Bb | |
| Gb | | | | Gb | Bb | Db |

Example 1d is similar to the previous example and uses the following sets of triads:

| Basic Chords | Am7 | Ab7 | GMaj7 |
|---|---|---|---|
| 1st Triad set | Am | Ab | G |
| 2nd Triad set | C | Cdim | Bm |
| 3rd Triad set | Em | Ebm | D |

In this example I play the triads in a pattern designed to make them fit the 1/8th note divisions of the 4/4 bar.

**Example 1d – Triad exercises through II V I with tritone substitution:**

*Am, Ab and G triads*

*C, Cdim and Bm triads*

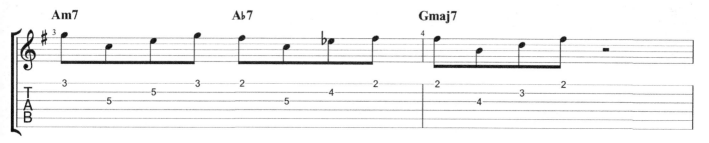

*Em, Ebm and D triads*

Explore this idea on your own and see how many variations you can come up with, using both the arpeggio and triad approaches. Focus on making smooth connections between the arpeggios / triads by keeping the movements as small as possible. Try composing a motif that you adjust slightly to fit each arpeggio / triad.

Example 1e uses the technique of drawing lines from the implied II chord of the dominant chord i.e. Ebm7 (II) lines over the Ab7 (V) chord.

This is a very useful substitution idea because you can, for instance, play a line over the Am7 chord then simply transpose the same line to Ebm7. Example 1e gives two examples of how this sounds.

**Example 1e**

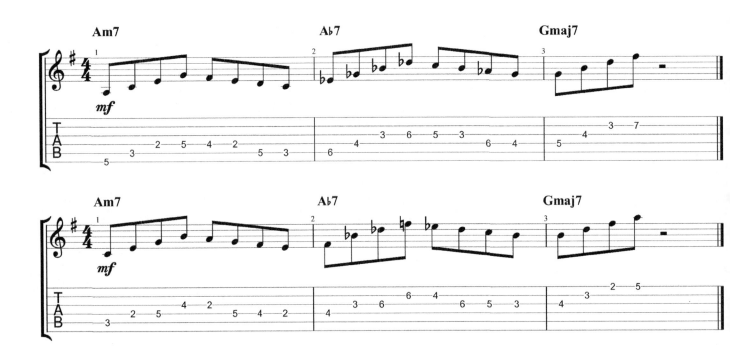

Now that you understand the most popular tritone ideas modern jazz players will use, let's learn some useful lick vocabulary to really embed this sound in your ears.

## Melodic Examples

The first example begins with a Cmaj7 arpeggio line (built from the 3rd degree of Am7) which creates an Am9 sound. I play a pull-off between the first two notes, but you could use legato on any part of the phrase. Experiment with your articulation to find your own unique approach.

The first part of the line over the Ab7 chord is an Ab7 scale run from root to 5th. I play a simple Ab7 arpeggio from the b7 to 5th. The notes C and Eb are used as chromatic approach notes to encircle the 5th of Gmaj7 (D) to resolve the phrase.

# Example 1f

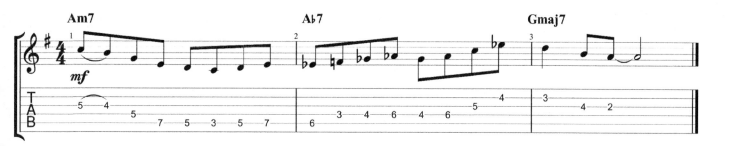

Example 1g begins with an Am7 scale fragment followed by a C major Coltrane pattern (1 2 3 5).

Until now, we have used arpeggios built on the root, 3rd, 5th and b7 degrees of the scale, but there are other options. Example 1g uses an Fm7 arpeggio over the Ab7 chord, built from the 6th degree of the Ab Mixolydian scale (F, Ab, C, Eb).

The line resolves to the 5th (D) of the Gmaj7 chord, before ascending an inversion of a Bm7 arpeggio to create a Gmaj9 sound.

# Example 1g

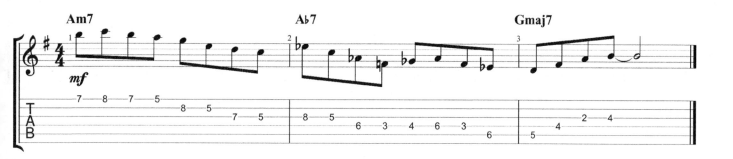

Tritone substitution is often associated with bebop and hardbop. Listen to the compositions of Wes Montgomery and Charlie Parker and you'll find examples where tritone II V lines appear where you normally expect to see just a dominant chord.

This idea also has a place in more modern types of jazz and can be combined with other ideas, such as using quartal arpeggios, shell voicings or triad pairs for a cutting-edge sound.

Example 1h features a Cmaj7 shell voicing arpeggio (C E B) over the Am7 chord. It's a sound associated with current modern jazz and you're unlikely to hear it in a Wes or Parker solo.

The line played over the Ab7 chord provides a contrast to the intervallic skips of the previous bar. It moves from F to Gb (AKA: F# the 3rd of D7) and descends the Ab Mixolydian scale before resolving to the 3rd (B) of Gmaj7.

Over the Gmaj7 chord there is a small arpeggio melody with a characteristic bebop skip at the end from F#
to D.

**Example 1h**

We'll return to the original II V I progression briefly to further explore the idea of playing minor arpeggios
over dominant chords – a strong idea in jazz soloing that you should definitely become accustomed to.

Refer back to the table of triad options and you'll see that Em is a good choice to play over an Am chord. In
Example 1i an ascending Em7 arpeggio is played over the Am7 chord, which encircles a C note (b3) on beat
3, before a small scale run descends from E to C.

The line played over the D7 chord combines two ideas. We've already discussed playing ideas based on the
II chord that could precede our b5 dominant chord (Ebm7 – Ab7). So, the first part of this line is an Ebm7
arpeggio. This is followed by an Fm7 arpeggio, which in the context of these chord changes can be seen as an
arpeggio built from the 3rd of D7. The F and the Eb notes work well to resolve to the 5th (D) of Gmaj7.

The final melodic fragment played over Gmaj7 is a Coltrane pattern from D, which is similar to the melody of
the jazz standard *Out of Nowhere*.

**Example 1i**

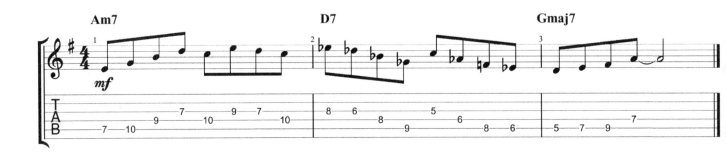

In Example 1j the first part of the lick over Am7 is a scale run that targets an Eb on beat 1 of the Ab7 chord.

The Ab7 line begins with a scale turn that highlights the b7 (Gb). From there it descends an Ebm7 arpeggio,
resolving from the low Eb to the 5th (D) of the Gmaj7 chord.

Over Gmaj7, the line concludes with a scale run that ends in a D major triad pattern (a major triad built from the 5th of the Imaj7 chord).

**Example 1j**

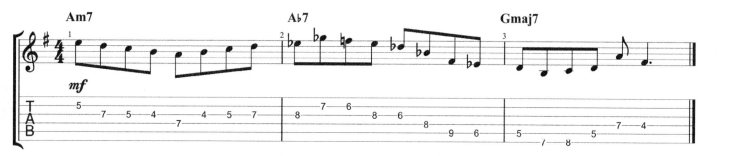

Another common soloing device in modern jazz is the minor pentatonic scale. In this example, the Am7 line uses shape two of the A Minor Pentatonic scale. It is a straightforward line and a good example of how to use this scale in a jazz context without sounding like a misplaced Eric Clapton!

Over the Ab7 chord an Ebm7 arpeggio is played and combined with a Gbmaj7 shell voicing (refer back to the "useful triads" table – the Gb major triad is built from the b7 of the Ab Mixolydian scale). This is a great way to highlight the 13th interval on the Ab7.

The 13th (F) resolves to the 5th (D) of Gmaj7 and the melody ends with a D major triad over the Gmaj7 chord.

**Example 1k**

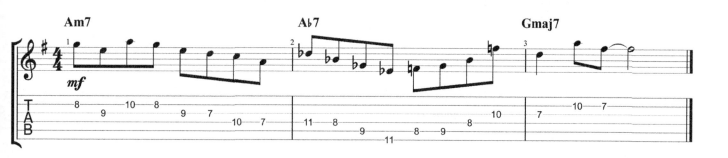

The use of quartal arpeggios is common in modern jazz. While there is a whole chapter dedicated to quartal harmony later in this book, I'll include one relevant example now, because it fits well with the tritone substitution concept.

In brief, traditional harmony is based on stacking notes in intervals of thirds, while quartal harmony stacks notes in fourths.

In Example 1l, a quartal arpeggio is played over the Am7 chord, starting on the highest C and skipping down to the lowest note before ascending. The second half of the bar is formed from an E minor Coltrane pattern (refer to my first book *Modern Jazz Guitar Concepts* for an in-depth discussion of Coltrane patterns).

The Ab7 line begins with a Gb triad with an F leading note. From beat 3, the line continues with a first inversion Cm7b5 arpeggio containing an Eb note that cleanly resolves to the 5th (D) of Gmaj7.

For the Gmaj7 chord, the line continues with a quartal arpeggio from B up to A. This could be viewed as coming from the B Minor Pentatonic scale. Playing a minor pentatonic scale built from the 3rd of a maj7 chord is a great substitution idea (in this case B Minor Pentatonic over Gmaj7). The table below illustrates why it works so well:

| Notes in B Minor Pentatonic | B | D | E | F# | A |
|---|---|---|---|---|---|
| Intervals formed over G Major | 3 | 5 | 6 (13) | 7 | 9 |

**Example 1l**

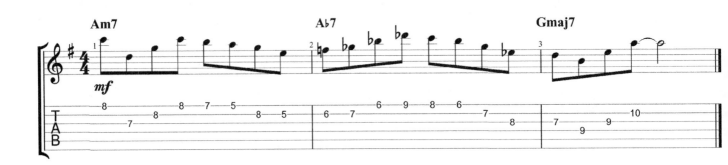

So far, we have discussed building lines based on common diatonic structures found in the Ab Mixolydian scale, but we can experiment with less common structures. Example 1m uses a sus4 triad built from the 4th degree of the scale: Dbsus4. Superimposed over our Ab7 chord, Dbsus4 gives the intervals: 4 (Db), b7 (Gb) and I (Ab).

Example 1m begins with a line combining a C Coltrane pattern and a scale run. In bar 2, an Eb minor triad is followed by a descending Dbsus4 triad. The effect of combining these triads suggests that the underlying harmony is an Ab7sus4 – which could also be viewed as Ebm11.

On beat 4 the notes C and Bb are used to chromatically approach the 3rd (B) of Gmaj7 before once again superimposing a Bm7 arpeggio.

**Example 1m**

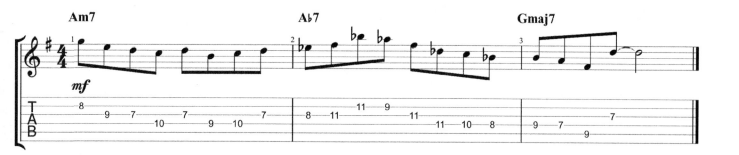

This lick combines the A Minor Pentatonic scale over the Am7 chord with a descending scale run from E to A.

The first part of Ab7 line is a quartal arpeggio played from Bb to Ab, followed by a descending scale run from Ab to C.

The line resolves from the note C to the 3rd (B) of Gmaj7. The final melodic tag is simply the major scale played in descending 3rds.

**Example 1n**

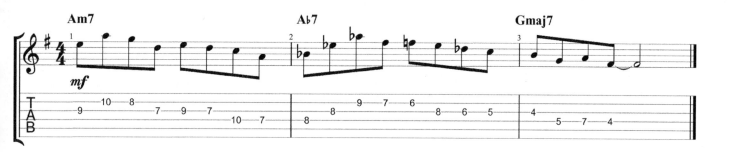

It's not common to hear an extended arpeggio played (i.e. one that includes all the upper extensions) in typical 1/8th note lines. More often, four-note arpeggios built on a particular chord tone are used to access the upper structures of chords. However, in this final example, I play a full Cmaj7(9) arpeggio (1, 3, 5, 7 and 9) on the Am7 chord for a bit of variation.

The Ab7 idea is once again based around an Ebm7 arpeggio, which creates an Ab7sus4 sound. Previously I resolved the suspension before moving to the Gmaj7 chord, but here I allow the Ab7sus4 sound to continue. The low Eb resolves to the 5th (D) of the Gmaj7 in a smooth, natural way before outlining a scale fragment from the B Minor Pentatonic scale.

# Example 1o

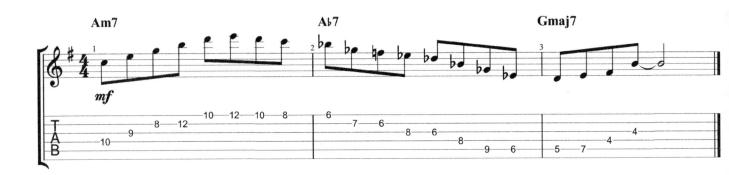

# Chapter Assignments

Write a set of five or more licks over a II V I progression in G using the following concepts:

- Play the Ab7 arpeggio as a tritone substitution.

- Play a Cm7b5 arpeggio over the Ab7.

- Experiment by creating an Ab7sus4 sound over the Ab7 using Ebm7 arpeggios, a Dbsus4 triad or Eb Minor Pentatonic scale.

- Keep a similar melodic shape between the Am7 and the Ab7 chords by "voice-leading" the melody. For example, playing an Am7 idea, then simply adjusting the notes to outline the Ab7 chord.

- Experiment playing Ab7 lines that use blues phrasing and pentatonic ideas to create another type of "blues sound" that can be used over a II V I in G Major.

- Solo by visualising and playing minor 7 chords built on the 5th degree of the II chord and the tritone substitution. For example: think Em7 over Am7, and Ebm7 over Ab7. You can use any minor ideas you know – such as the Dorian scale, triads, arpeggios or pentatonic scales. For bonus points, you can resolve these ideas to a D major triad over the Gmaj7 chord.

- When you're confident playing in the key of G, explore the keys of Bb, Eb and C Major.

# Chapter Two: Triad Pairs in the Altered Scale

Improvising by combining triad pairs is a common device in modern jazz soloing. This technique can be used on all types of chords, but since this book focuses on the II V I sequence, it makes sense to apply the concept to altered dominant chords.

Improvising with triad pairs simply means to isolate two triads from a parent scale and use them as melodic material for soloing. This works well because triads are strong melodic structures that stand out to the listener. By splitting melodies between two separate triads you instantly create a set of changing colours that emphasise different intervals over the underlying chord.

The Melodic Minor scale is more forgiving than the major scale in this regard. You have to be quite selective when experimenting with triad pairs in major scale harmony, but with the melodic minor it's fine to play *any arpeggio* from the scale over any of the chords in the scale and it will always sound great. For this reason, we'll use melodic minor triad pairs.

In this chapter, the II V I sequence is in the key of F Major: Gm7 – C7 – Fmaj7.

The most common melodic minor scale to play over the C7 chord is C Altered – the seventh mode of the Db Melodic Minor scale.

**Side note:** *The Db Melodic Minor scale contains the somewhat confusing and un-guitaristic 'Fb' note. When it occurs, I've rewritten it as an E. It's easier to read and E is also the 3rd of C7.*

Taking the same approach as the previous chapter, explore one position of the C7 Altered scale.

**Example 2a**

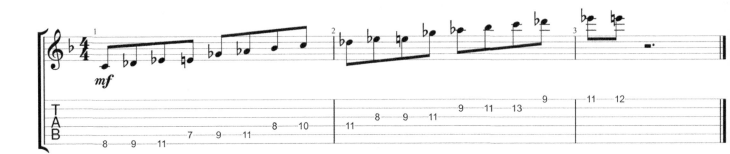

Now let's look at the triads available in the Db Melodic Minor (C Altered) scale.

**Example 2b**

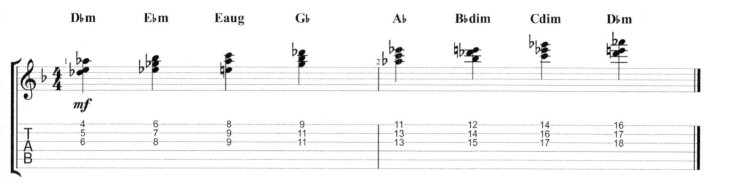

The available triads are:

| Dbm | Ebm | Eaug | GbMaj | AbMaj | Bbdim | Cdim |
|-----|-----|------|-------|-------|-------|------|

Here we encounter diminished and augmented triads for the first time. They are built as follows:

Diminished (dim) = 1 b3 b5

Augmented (aug) = 1 3 #5

Put simply, a triad *pair* just means two triads located a tone apart i.e. Dbm and Ebm. When combined, any two triads that don't contain common notes, will contain six different pitches. In other words, all of the notes in the scale except one.

In total, you will find seven different triad pairs in the scale which don't share any common notes, and which are adjacent to each other in the scale. This might sound more like science than music to you, but the table below makes it easier to understand:

| Triad One | Triad Two |
|-----------|-----------|
| Dbm (Db, E, Ab) | Ebm (Eb, Gb, Bb) |
| Ebm (Eb, Gb, Bb) | Eaug (E, G#/Ab, C) |
| Eaug (E, G#/Ab, C) | GbMaj (Gb, Bb, Db) |
| GbMaj (Gb, Bb, Db) | AbMaj (Ab, C, Eb) |
| AbMaj (Ab, C, Eb) | Bbdim (Bb, Db, E) |
| Bbdim (Bb, Db, E) | Cdim (C, Eb, Gb) |
| Cdim (C, Eb, Gb) | Dbm (Db, Eb, Ab) |

When we play these triad pairs in a solo, they are always heard as *upper structures* (intervals higher than an octave, i.e., 9, 11, and 13), and it is important to understand how the notes in each triad relate to the root of the C7alt chord.

Here are the notes of Db Melodic Minor superimposed over a C7 chord:

| Db Melodic Minor Scale | Db | Eb | E | Gb | Ab | Bb | C |
|---|---|---|---|---|---|---|---|
| **Relation to C7** | b9 | #9 | 3 | #11 | b13 | b7 | 1 |

The following table shows the effect each *triad* has when played over C7. So, if you wanted to emphasise a #9 and #11 tonality, you could choose to play an Ebm triad over C7, for instance.

| **Dbm** | Db, E, Ab | b9,3,b13 |
|---|---|---|
| **Ebm** | Eb, Gb, Bb | #9,#11,b7 |
| **Eaug** | E, Ab, C | 3,b13,1 |
| **GbMaj** | Gb, Bb, Db | #11,b7,b9 |
| **AbMaj** | Ab, C, Eb | b13, 1,#9 |
| **Bbdim** | Bb, Db, E | b7,b9,3 |
| **Cdim** | C, Eb, Gb | 1,#9,#11 |

## Practicing Triad Pairs

Having laid the foundation for the theory, the best way to get to grips with triad pairs is to hear how they sound against the chords. The following exercises begin with general exercises for practising triads and move on to explore specific triad pair ideas.

Let's begin with some common patterns to play triads, which will allow you to create a vast number of amount of melodies.

The first exercise is built around the Dbm triad and its inversions. They are written in triplets to make it easier to see the different inversions. This will be useful later when the triads pairs are combined.

**Example 2c – Dbm Triad Inversions:**

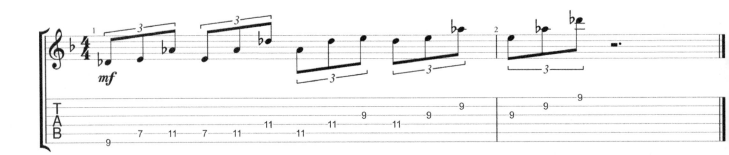

Now vary this pattern by playing the root position triad ascending and the next inversion descending:

**Example 2d**

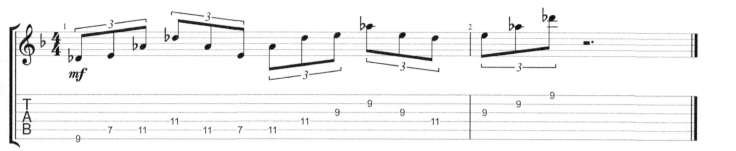

Here's an important approach that uses note "skipping". Instead of a 1 3 5 pattern, it is now 1 5 3 (root, fifth, third).

**Example 2e**

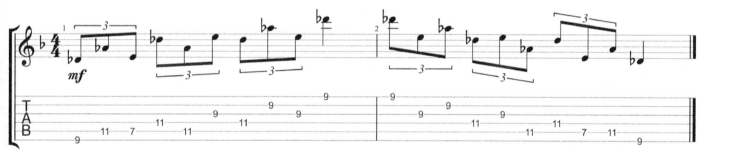

These exercises should get the sound of the triad into your head. Once you have learnt the patterns, over time work to apply them to all the diatonic triads of Db Melodic Minor and you will begin to build a vocabulary for improvising with triad pairs.

Now let's combine two triads and work towards soloing with triad pairs. The next examples combine the Dbm and Ebm triads. In Example 2f, play through the triad inversions which alternate between Dbm and Ebm.

**Example 2f**

Example 2g alternates between Dbm and Ebm triads, ascending and descending. This will develop your flexibility and help you connect the triads in a more creative way.

**Example 2g**

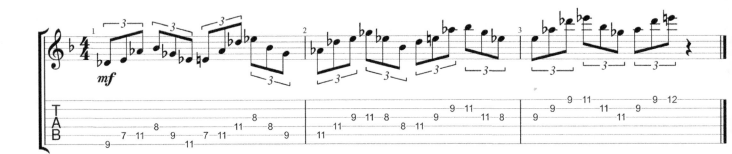

You can also change the note order for each inversion, as in Example 2e. Here we begin on the second note instead of the root. The 1 3 5 pattern becomes 3 1 5 and this continues through the sequence.

**Example 2h**

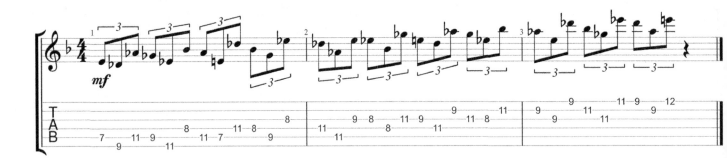

The final exercise is an example of how you might freely connect the triads using all the above patterns and inversions to create a melody with many skips and surprising intervals.

**Example 2i – Improvising with the Triad Inversions:**

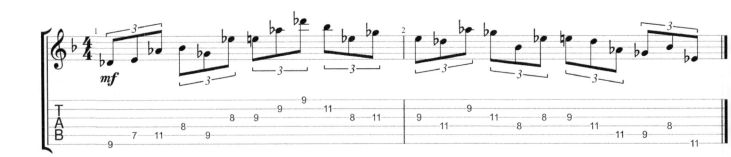

## Triad Pair Licks

Now that we have some material to use on the C7alt chord we can start to play it over the II V7alt I sequence in F Major. The following lick examples explore the melodic possibilities using triad pairs from the C Altered (Db Melodic Minor) scale.

In Example 2j, the line played over Gm7 (chord II) combines an ascending Dm7 arpeggio with a descending 1 2 3 5 Gm arpeggio pattern. Playing a diatonic arpeggio from the 5th of the chord (Dm7 arpeggio over Gm7) is a useful approach in almost any context.

The line for the C7alt chord is two major triads a whole step apart. In the C Altered scale, these occur on the b5 and b6 of the scale: Gb major and Ab major.

The line resolves to the 9th (G) of Fmaj7.

**Example 2j**

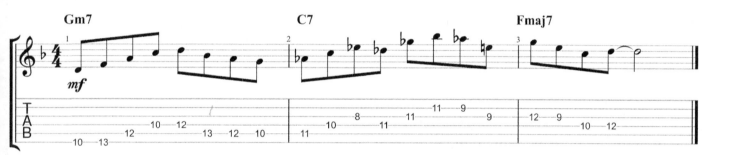

In the next example, the Gm7 line begins with a descending scale fragment that continues into the first inversion of a Bbmaj7 arpeggio.

Over C7alt, the triad pair of Eaug and Gbmaj really convey the altered scale sound, as they contain the 3rd and b7 guide tones of the C7 chord (Bb and E), along with some tasty alterations. The augmented triad strongly colours the melody.

The melodic line ends with a more open-ended sounding statement over the Fmaj7, which consists of a quartal arpeggio (stacked fourths) beginning on an A note, followed by a scale run and a beautiful diatonic 6th skip up to the C.

**Example 2k**

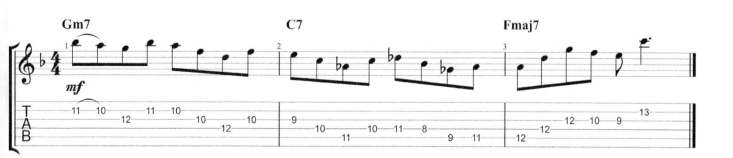

In this example, the opening statement is similar to the previous lick, but this time the Bbmaj7 line is played in first inversion.

The triad pair played over C7 is formed from Dbm and Ebm, with the Dm triad in second inversion. The resolution to Fmaj7 is via a leading note that targets the 3rd (A).

The line finishes with a melody based around the first inversion C major triad (again, using the arpeggio based on the 5th of the Fmaj7 chord).

**Example 2l**

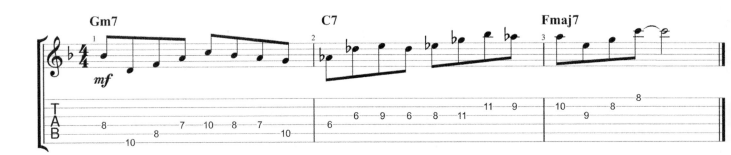

This example uses the root of Gm7 as a leading note into a descending Bbmaj7 arpeggio. This is a strong melodic idea that you should turn into an exercise by taking it through the whole scale.

The triad pair over C7 is Abmaj and Bbdim. The Abmaj triad is played in root position; the Bbdim is in first inversion and resolves to the 3rd (A) of Fmaj7.

The final part of the lick is a descending A Minor Pentatonic scale run ending on the 6th (D) of Fmaj7.

**Example 2m**

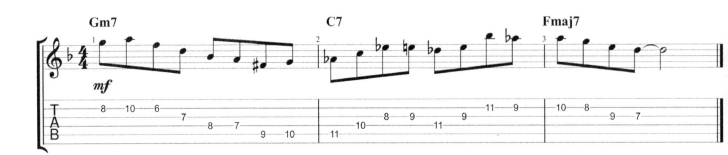

Sus4 triads are great to use on many different chords. Here I use a Dsus4 triad over the Gm7 chord to target the 3rd (Bb). From there it skips up to C and continues with a descending scale run.

The C7alt line is a triad pattern based on the first inversion of Abmaj. The pattern repeats with a Gbmaj triad played in root position, to bring out the larger intervals in the line. The line resolves to the 3rd (A) of Fmaj7 and ends with an Fmaj7 shell voicing.

**Example 2n**

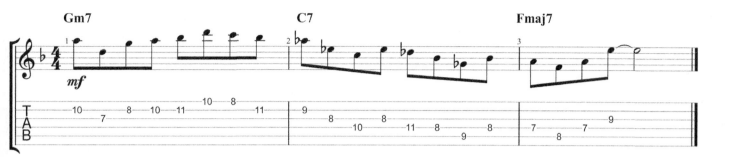

The next example builds an idea with a large melodic range. The Gm7 line begins with a small descending scale fragment before continuing with a quartal arpeggio built from the 5th (D).

This example returns to the Eaug and Gbmaj triad pair over C7alt, which is one of my favourite sounds. I like it because of the striking sound of the augmented triad, and because Gbmaj emphasises the b5 (Gb) of the C7 chord.

The first triad is Gbmaj played in first inversion, before the Eaug triad is played descending. The line resolves to the 3rd (A) of Fmaj7 and continues into an Am7 arpeggio.

**Example 2o**

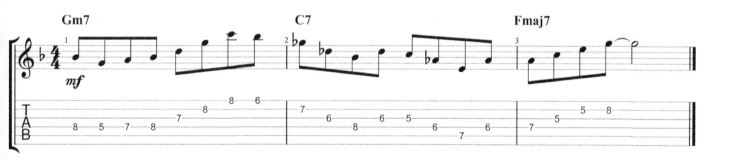

In Example 2p, the Gm7 line is constructed from Gm and Bbmaj arpeggios, both beginning on the 5th. For the C7alt chord, a Gbmaj triad links to an ascending Abmaj triad in first inversion, which resolves to the 9th (G) of Fmaj7.

**Example 2p**

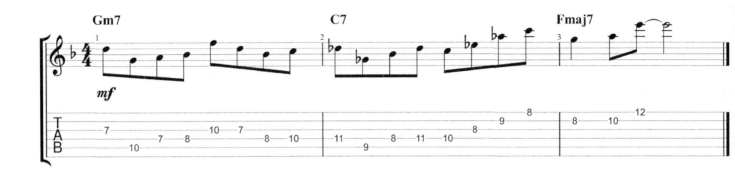

The next idea begins with a popular Coltrane pattern (an arpeggio played with a 1 2 3 5 sequence) then continues down the Gm Pentatonic scale.

The line over C7alt begins with a first inversion Bbdim triad followed by a root position Abmaj triad. This resolves to the 3rd (A) of the Fmaj7 and ends with a descending Cmaj triad.

**Example 2q**

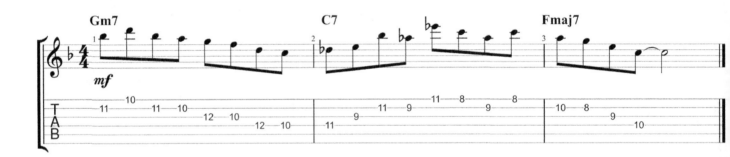

In Example 2r, a quartal arpeggio built on the 5th (D) works well in combination with a Bbmaj triad over the Gm7 chord. The top note of the quartal arpeggio is used as a part of an enclosure that targets the Bb note. The triad is played as a 1 5 3 pattern to add an interesting ascending 5th interval to the lick.

The C7alt line is constructed from an Eaug and Ebm triad pair. Each triad is played with a pattern that allows it to last for four notes. The line resolves to the 9th (G) of Fmaj7 and finishes with a descending Cmaj Coltrane pattern.

**Example 2r**

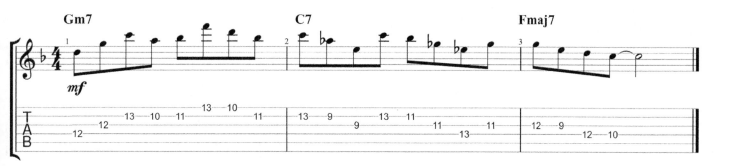

Playing arpeggios in set patterns is an easy and practical way to add large interval skips to your solos. The final example starts with a Bbmaj7 arpeggio played with the sequence: 3, 1, 5, 3, 7. This is followed by a Gm triad.

Over the C7 chord I have once again used the triad pair of Abmaj then Gbmaj. The resolution to Fmaj7 is achieved with a quick b9, #9 turn that resolves to the 7th (E).

The final part of the lick is a descending Am triad that skips up to the 6th (D) of Fmaj7.

**Example 2s**

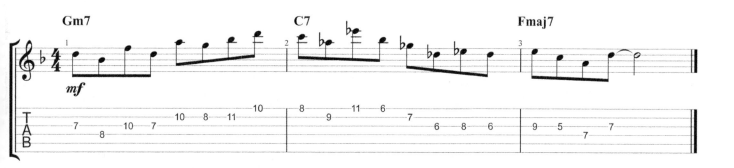

# Chapter Assignments

Write a set of five or more licks over a progression, or compose a short solo over a song using:

- The Eaug an Gbmaj triad pair.

- Construct motif-based melodies on the entire II V I by using Abmaj and Bbmaj triad pairs on the II chord and Eaug and Gbmaj on the V7alt chord.

- Use patterns beyond simple inversions on the triad pairs to connect them in other ways and expand how you can play melodies with triads.

- Avoid changing direction when moving from one triad to the next to practise creating lines with a larger, more dramatic range.

- Explore the Gbmaj and Abmaj triad pairs using patterns as in Example 2h.

- Construct motif-based melodies over the entire II V I sequence using Bbmaj and Cmaj on the II chord and Gbmaj and Abmaj on the V7alt chord.

- Work with the Eaug and Gbmaj triads to really dig into the sound of the augmented triad on an altered dominant chord.

- Create cascading melodies similar to Example 2n to create lines with shifting colours on top of the chord.

# Chapter Three: Quartal Arpeggios

Quartal harmony is a great way to get new sounds into your playing. As you probably know, traditional harmony builds chords by stacking thirds. For example, the chord of Cmaj7 is built by stacking the 3rd intervals C, E, G and B. Quartal harmony is based on stacking fourths and the same chord is built C, F, B and E. This creates a completely different sound – one which conjures up a very different mood, because your ears are accustomed to hearing harmony based on thirds.

Quartal harmony was brought to a jazz audience in the late 1950s when Miles Davis and Bill Evans used it on the iconic album, *Kind of Blue*. This became the signature sound of much of the modal jazz of the 1960s and was intrinsic to the styles of pianist McCoy Tyner and saxophonist John Coltrane. It was also explored in the harmonic vocabulary of musicians such as Herbie Hancock, Wayne Shorter and Joe Henderson.

## Basic Quartal Harmony Theory

If you are not familiar with hearing quartal harmony, at first it may sound exotic and strange. Despite not containing traditional third-based chords, we don't actually change the harmony of the song when replacing the original chords with their quartal equivalents. Instead, we use the concept to create spacious sounding chords to spell out the existing changes. The effect is to use the open sound of the quartal chords to add another colour to the harmony.

The way we use quartal arpeggios is similar. You can use them to create a different set of notes, which are still related to the chords, from which you can create melodies.

Let's have a look at how this works for an Am7 chord in the key of C Major. The first line shows the traditional Am7 arpeggio built in 3rds. Below it is an Am7 arpeggio is built in 4ths.

| Am7 in 3rds | A | C | E | G |
| Am7 in 4ths | A | D | G | C |

The difference in sound between the chords is not so much because of the notes – only two differ (D and E), and both chords contain the important guide tones b3 (C) and b7 (G). The difference in sound is due to the *spacing of the intervals* between the notes.

Play both chords on the guitar. They are voiced from the lowest to highest note. The first one might be a bit of a stretch, but the comparison will help you hear how quartal harmony sounds compared to the traditional chord in thirds.

**Example 3a – Am7 stacked 3rds; Am7 stacked 4ths (Am11)**

Am7                                    Am7(11)

Quartal chords have an open, ambiguous sound to them and, because they are built in fourths, have a strong connection to suspended chords. The first inversion of a Sus4 triad, for instance, forms a (quartal) Sus2 stack of 4ths. The second inversion of the Sus4 chord is a three-note quartal voicing of a D chord. (See table below).

| Root Position | First Inversion | Second Inversion |
|---------------|-----------------|------------------|
| Gsus4 | Csus2 | D quartal chord |
| G | C | D |
| C | D | G |
| D | G | C |

**Example 3b – related triads: Gsus4, Csus4 and DMaj7 (quartal chord)**

Gsus4                    Csus2                    D quartal chord

## Building a Vocabulary of Quartal Arpeggios

Quartal chords don't have a clear root note, like chords made from stacked thirds, and each voicing could be interpreted as several different chords. In this chapter we will focus on developing a vocabulary around three-note quartal arpeggios, which are easy structures to play and use over other chords. I have chosen to teach you these voicings on the middle strings for the following reasons:

- It's likely you've come across similar voicings to these chords before

- They are easier to play than on other string groupings

- This register is perfect for lines and voicings using quartal structures

## The Major Scale

The best way to begin to understand quartal harmony is to hear it in action, so let's learn a set of quartal chord voicings that we will then turn into arpeggios. Play through Example 3c – diatonic stacks of 4ths built from the C Major scale, played on the middle string set.

**Example 3c**

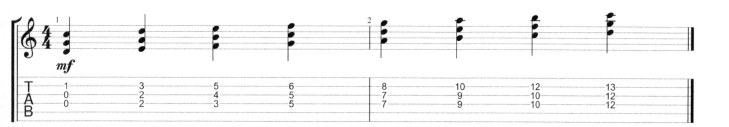

The chords can now be played arpeggios as follows.

**Example 3d**

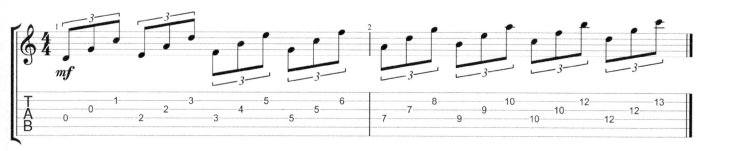

I'm sure you noticed that two chords in the previous two examples were fingered slightly different from all the others. These chords need a bit of extra attention because they contain tritone (#4 = b5) intervals between two of their notes. This happens on chord I (C) and chord IV (F).

The I chord (C = C, F, B) contains a tritone between the second two notes F and B.

The IV chord (F = F, B, E) contains a tritone between the first two notes, F and B.

Both chords have a few specific applications that will prove useful later.

The easiest way to get started making music with quartal arpeggios is to learn them along a string set as shown above, but you should also learn them in fixed scale positions too.

The next example shows how to play diatonic quartal arpeggios in the 8th position. This is challenging, but it's important to learn them around their parent major scale, and where they will be played on the guitar neck

**Example 3e**

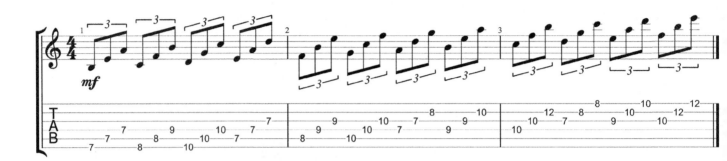

## Melodic Minor and The Altered Scale

Now let's learn the quartal chords and arpeggios in the melodic minor scale. This is a logical step because it's a common jazz scale and the parent scale of the all-important Altered scale that we play on the V chord of the II V I.

Again, we will learn the voicings on a three-string set and then use them to form arpeggios. The musical examples later in this chapter are played over a II V I progression in C Major (Dm7 – G7 – Cmaj7), so we will use the Ab Minor Melodic scale, the parent of the G Altered scale.

**Example 3f**

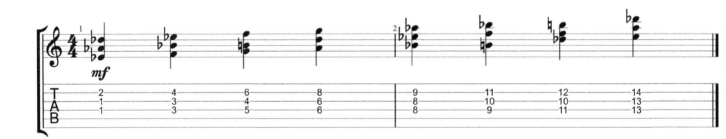

These voicings can now be turned into arpeggios.

**Example 3g**

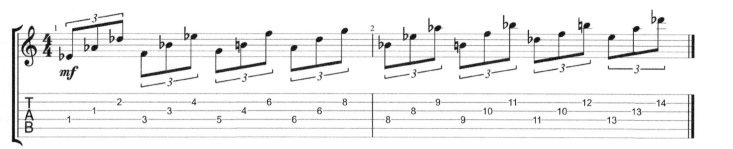

As you played through the melodic minor quartal voicings in examples 3f and 3g, you may have found it hard to recognise some of them as quartal structures because they contain a 3rd interval. Let's have a closer look at those.

Look at the 7th degree of the quartal harmonised Ab Melodic Minor scale and you'll see it forms a G7 shell voicing of G, B and F (the 1, 3 and b7 *guide tones* of a G7).

The quartal arpeggio on the note B (the 3rd of G Altered) contains the notes B, F and A#(Bb). This spells out the 3, b7 and #9 extension of a G7#9 chord.

The Db quartal arpeggio Db, G, B could be rearranged as a Gmaj b5 triad (G, B, Db) as a great sound to play over G7alt.

Example 3h will help you to practise these arpeggios across the fretboard. When you are comfortable with this exercise, learn to play them in one position on the neck. This will help your soloing fluency and get the intervals under your fingers.

**Example 3h**

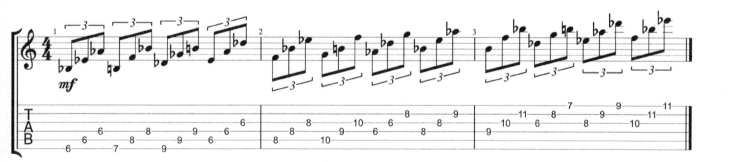

## Quartal Arpeggio Musical Examples

The examples in this section apply three-note quartal arpeggios as part of some modern jazz lines. Some are played on the II chord and some on the altered V chord of the II V I sequence (Dm7, G7alt, Cmaj7).

In Example 3i, the line played over Dm7 begins with a double chromatic enclosure that targets the b3 (F) before descending a Dm7 arpeggio.

Two quartal arpeggios are used on the G7alt chord. The first, built on the 3rd (B) contains the notes B, F and Bb (A#). You might recognise this arpeggio as the upper part of the G7(#9) chord described above. The second is built on an Eb (b13). This arpeggio (Eb, Ab, Db) consists solely of the alterations b13, b9 and b5. The altered dominant line resolves to the 9th (D) of Cmaj7.

**Example 3i**

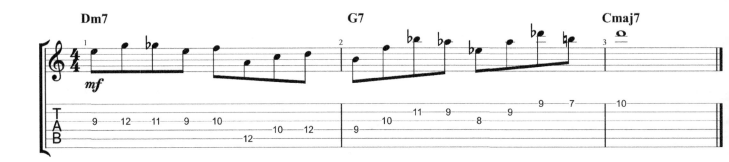

The next idea begins with the same double chromatic approach used above to target the F (b3) on beat 3, then descends an Fmaj7 arpeggio to imply a Dm9 sound.

The G7 line combines two quartal arpeggios. The first one is built on the second chord of the Ab Melodic Minor scale (or #9 of the G Altered scale) Bb, Eb, Ab. These notes create #9, b13 and b9 intervals against the G7 chord. The next is built from B, B, F, Bb, just like the previous lick. Both ascend and syncopate the flow of the lines nicely with two groups of three notes played against the 4/4 time.

The Ab and the F at the end of the phrase resolve the line to the 5th (G) of Cmaj7.

**Example 3j**

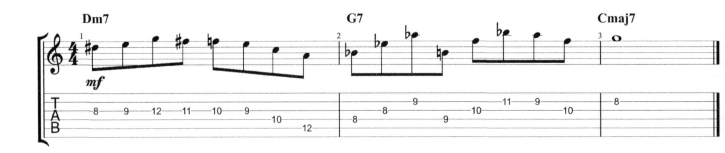

In Example 3k, E and C# form a chromatic approach pattern to encircle the root of Dm7. The line continues with a common four-note 1 2 3 5 arpeggio pattern on the Dm7. The melody moves chromatically to the b7 (F) on G7.

Again, for the G7 chord, the melodic line is formed from two quartal arpeggios and two notes that smoothly resolve to the Cmaj7 chord. Even though the basic idea is identical, this is a good example of how much variation exists inside the same structure.

The first quartal arpeggio is built on F (b7) (F, Bb, Eb) which offers the intervals b7, #9 and b13 over the G7 chord. The next quartal arpeggio is built on Bb (#9) (Bb, Eb, Ab) to introduce the only new note (Ab) as a b9 extension. From the Ab the line descends step-wise to resolve to the 3rd (E) of Cmaj7.

**Example 3k**

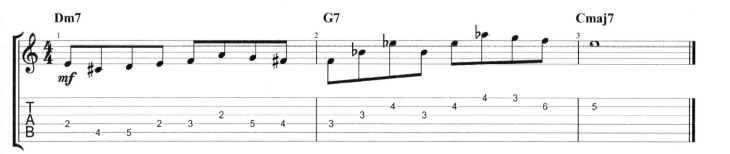

You can also use quartal arpeggios on the IIm7 chord, and the next idea begins with a line over Dm7 constructed from quartal arpeggios. Each arpeggio is played descending, which gives the first (and highest) note in each group of three an accent. The successive groups of three notes against the 1/8th note subdivisions create a strong polyrhythmic element to the melody.

Three quartal arpeggios are used over Dm7, the first notes of each forming an ascending step-wise melody of F, G and A. The transition to the G7alt chord is achieved by shifting the final arpeggio down a half step to become the quartal arpeggio Bb, Eb, Ab.

The ascending movement continues through B, F and Bb and before finally resolving via Ab to the 5th (G) of Cmaj7.

**Example 3l**

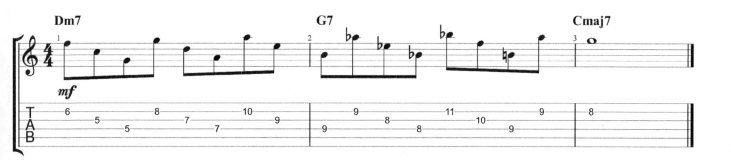

When quartal chords are used in comping, the rhythm player often shifts the chords up and down the neck in a stepwise manner. A classic example of is the rhythm part to Miles Davis' *So What*. This approach occurs in much of McCoy Tyner's comping with John Coltrane too. A melodic version of this approach is used over the G7 chord in this example.

The Dm7 line starts with a chromatic approach from G to F before the jump up to A. This fragment might just be one of the most common bebop phrases in existence. From there the melody skips down to an E and ascends towards an F on the G7 chord.

The two quartal arpeggios on the G7 are built from structures a whole step apart: the b7 (F) and the b13 (Eb). These two arpeggios contain five of the seven notes in the G Altered scale, only missing the G and B. The line uses the #9 and b9 to resolve to the 5th (G) of Cmaj7.

**Example 3m**

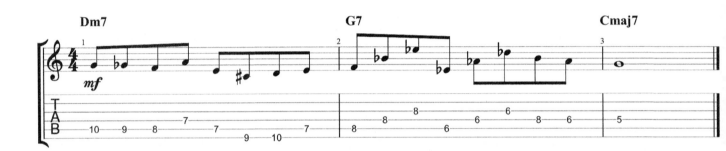

The next lick demonstrates another way to combine two quartal arpeggios on the V7 chord. Here they are placed on beats 1 and 3, the strongest beats in the bar, with a note added to transition from one to the next.

The foundation of the Dm7 line is a Dm triad in first inversion (F, A, D), but starts with an E approach note. The line moves to the G7 chord via a three-note chromatic enclosure to target the 3rd (B) of G7.

Once on the G7 chord, a quartal arpeggio from B links to the next quartal arpeggio built from F. It resolves to the 9th (D) of Cmaj7.

**Example 3n**

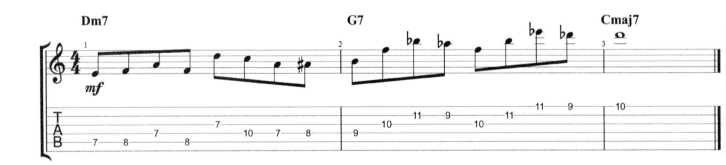

Until now the quartal arpeggios have been played with just one note per string. This makes it easy to relate them to their chord voicings, but can present challenges in terms of right hand technique. In this example, the altered dominant line uses an arpeggio played on a two string set. 4th intervals played on the same string can be a bit of a stretch but playing them like this is a decent trade-off between right- and left-hand techniques.

The two-string voicing of the quartal arpeggio is built on the note F (F, Bb, Eb). This is followed by a one note per string version built on Eb (Eb, Ab, Db). The line resolves to the 5th (G) of Cmaj7.

**Example 3o**

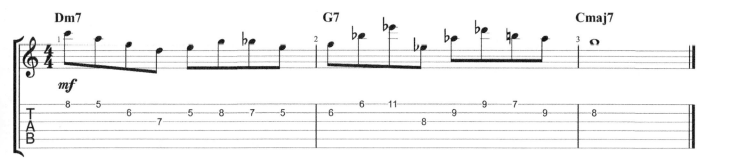

This example uses quartal arpeggios on both the IIm7 and the V7 chord.

The Dm7 line starts with a Dm triad which connects nicely to a quartal arpeggio build on G (4th) (G, C, F). From the F it skips down to D and ascends the scale to target the b7 (F) on the G7.

Over the G7 chord, the first structure is an F quartal arpeggio (F, Bb, Eb) to highlight the b7, #9 and b13 of the G7alt chord. This is then connected to a Db7 arpeggio inversion to create a Db7 Lydian Dominant (G Altered) sound (Db7 is the tritone substitution of G7). The descending Db7 arpeggio neatly resolves to the 5th (G) of Cmaj7.

**Example 3p**

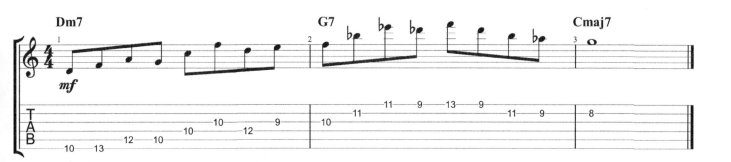

For Example 3q, over the Dm7 chord the lick descends an Am Coltrane pattern and continues with a quartal arpeggio built on G (4th). The combination of 11 (G), b7 (C) and b3 (F) intervals creates a Dm7(11) sound. The Dm7 line is extended across the bar line into the G7 bar using another quartal arpeggio built from A (A, D, F).

This lick does not introduce the altered scale until beat 2 of the second bar. The entire G7 line then consists of two quartal arpeggios, one built from Bb (Bb, Eb, Ab) and one built from B (B, F, Bb) to create a G7b9b13 sound. The final arpeggio resolves to the 7th (B) of the Cmaj7.

**Example 3q**

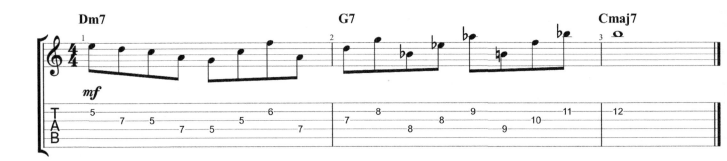

In this final example the arpeggios are chained together to create a large musical range from low to high.

The line over Dm7 begins with a quartal arpeggio built from D (D, G, C), and continues with a quartal arpeggio built from A (A, D, G).

The line over G7 uses the same pattern on the quartal arpeggio, built from Bb, and is followed by an upper-structure triad of Ab minor. This arpeggio encircles and resolves the line to the 9th (D) of Cmaj7.

**Example 3r**

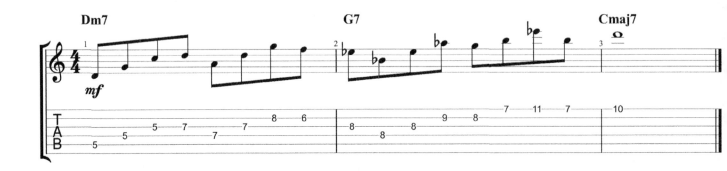

# Chapter Assignments

Write a set of five or more licks over a progression, or a short solo over a song using:

- Step-wise motion in quartal arpeggios, as in Example 3m

- Chaining together quartal arpeggios as in Example 3r

- Using cascading arpeggios as in Example 3l

The important thing when trying to write lines with this material is to figure out which quartal arpeggios you like to use over the chords, then to work at combining them with vocabulary your already know (such as triads, seventh chord arpeggios and licks).

Use the table below to identify what interval each note of the quartal arpeggio forms against the chords.

**Side note:** It makes sense to view the G as an 11th against the Dm7 chord, because Dm11 is a common chord sound. For the G7 and Cmaj7 chords the 11th is not a common extension, so here I have called it a 4th. This is particularly useful on the G7, as you'll learn to use the quartal arpeggios to convey a useful G7sus4 sound.

| Arpeggio | Dm7 | G7 | CMaj7 |
|---|---|---|---|
| C, F, B | b7, b3, 13 | 4, b7, 3 | 1, 4, 7 |
| D, G, C | 1, 11, b7 | 5, 1, 4 | 9, 5, 1 |
| E, A, D | 9, 5, 1 | 13, 9, 5 | 3, 13, 9 |
| F, B, E | b3, 13, 9 | b7, 3, 13 | 4, 7, 3 |
| G, C, F | 11, b7, b3 | 1, 4, b7 | 5, 1, 4 |
| A, D, G | 5, 1, 11 | 9, 5, 1 | 13, 2, 5 |
| B, E, A | 13, 9, 5 | 3, 13, 9 | 7, 3, 13 |

On G7alt we use the following quartal arpeggios from the Ab Melodic Minor / G Altered scale:

| Quartal Arpeggio from G Altered | Interval Against G7 |
|---|---|
| G, B, F | 1, 3, b7 |
| Ab, Db, G | b9, b5, 1 |
| Bb, Eb, Ab | #9, b13, b9 |
| B, F, Bb | 3, b7, #9 |
| Db, G, B | b5, 1, 3 |
| Eb, Ab, Db | b13, b9, b5 |
| F, Bb, Eb | b7, #9, b13 |

Try these out in a few common guitar keys to help you internalise the relationships between quartal arpeggios and the intervals they create over common chords.

# Chapter Four: Intervallic Structures

As guitarists, it can be difficult to play large interval skips in solos, but this skill is essential to avoid simply running up and down scales. One way to solve this problem is to use the larger intervals found in chord shapes that you already know. Since these voicings already sound good as chords, they automatically create strong melodies.

In this chapter you will learn how to convert chord voicings you know into arpeggios structures you can use in your solos. We will explore this technique using both drop 2 chords and shell (root and guide tone) voicings. You can use a similar approach to explore drop3, drop 2&4 and any other type of chord voicing you may wish to use.

This approach has been important since the 1960s and there are examples of Jimmy Raney experimenting with arpeggiated chord voicings in his solos. It is also a device commonly used by saxophone players and is heard often in the playing of the likes of Michael Brecker, Chris Potter and Mark Turner.

Personally, I find that drop 2 chords and shell voicings create wonderful arpeggios that introduce greater range and larger intervals into my solos, which helps me play more interesting and surprising lines.

The examples and exercises in this chapter are all in the key of Bb Major. Note that the exercises don't always begin on the note Bb, because this allows us to access the full range of the guitar.

Most of the voicings are played as one note per string patterns, because that's how they're played as chords. Consequently, playing these arpeggios can be quite demanding for you right hand and it's best to use strict alternate picking. Checking out picking exercises by players like Steve Morse and other Bluegrass-inspired guitarists will help a lot. Either way, you'll find that the exercises in this chapter serve as good workouts for your right hand precision and speed.

## Drop 2 Voicings

One of the most common ways to make seventh chords playable on guitar is to use drop 2 voicings. You will already know a few of them, even if you are not familiar with the term drop 2 voicings.

A seventh chord is formed from four notes of a scale stacked in 3rds. For example, Bbmaj7 = Bb, D, F A.

Look at Example 4a below. In bar one, a *closed* voicing of the Bbmaj7 chord is shown. The voicing is a straight stack of 3rds from root to 7th.

In bar two, the second highest note (F) is dropped down an octave to create a drop 2 voicing.

Drop 2 literally means "drop the second highest note in a closed voicing down an octave".

As you can see, the first drop 2 voicing doesn't contain a note on the B string, which makes this voicing difficult to play, but it can be re-fingered to play all four notes on adjacent strings to make it easier (see the second chord in bar two). Check out the notation above the tablature. You'll see that both chords are identical, just re-fingered for playability.

**Example 4a**

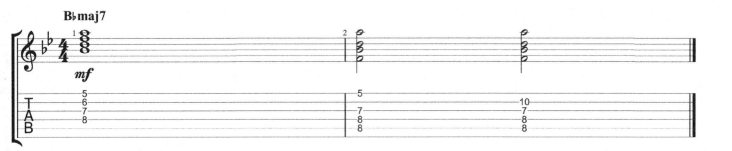

The previous example shows how drop 2 voicings are constructed, but it doesn't necessarily explain why we do this. Simply put, on guitar it is difficult to play *inversions* of 7th chords because they always contain wide stretches.

Drop 2 voicings not only sound great, they fix the stretching problem by making inversions of 7th chords much more playable on guitar. If you listen to Wes Montgomery's chord solos, you will hear drop 2 voicings and inversions being played almost exclusively.

## Drop 2 Voicing Exercises with Arpeggios

Drop 2 voicings are usually played on four adjacent strings:

Low: E, A, D, G strings

Middle: A, D, G, B strings

High: D, G, B, E. strings

As an introduction let's learn the diatonic drop 2 voicings in Bb Major, where the root is played on the lowest string. If you want to dig a little deeper into this, you can explore the other inversions yourself and put those into exercises.

In Example 4b, the diatonic chords of Bb Major are played on the lowest string set. Since the lowest available note in this key on this string is an F, the first chord is an F7. The chords then move up through the Bb Major scale diatonically to the F an octave above.

Practise this as both the written arpeggios, but strummed as complete chords too. I am quite convinced that it is impossible to practise too many diatonic chord voicings!

**Example 4b**

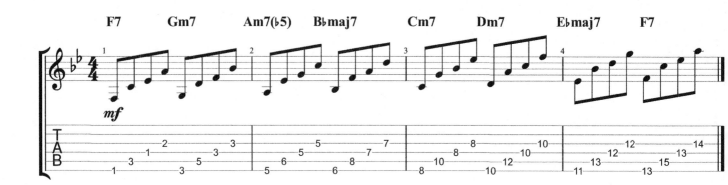

The second exercise is the same concept played on the middle string set. The lowest note available is the root of the Bb Major scale. Again, play these as both chords and arpeggios.

**Example 4c**

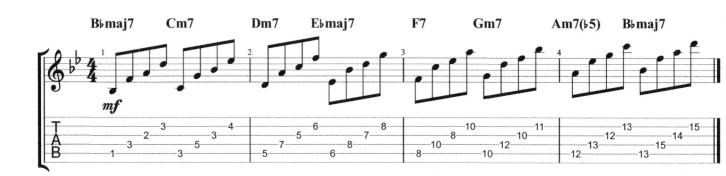

The high string set will probably prove most useful when using drop 2 chords for comping, and they are very useful when soloing with drop 2 arpeggios.

The lowest available root note in Bb Major on the 4th string is Eb, so the first voicing in this diatonic set is the Ebmaj7 chord.

**Example 4d**

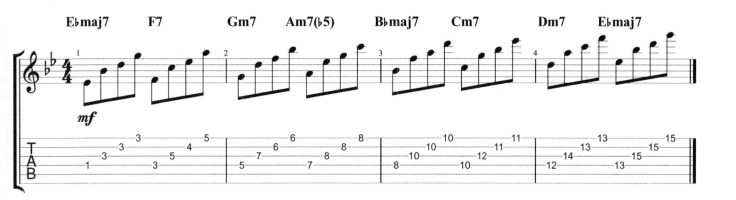

## Phrasing and Technique Choices

The most difficult part of playing these arpeggios is finding a right-hand technique that works. Since these arpeggios are arranged one note per string, it's tempting to use sweeping or economy picking. I find that these approaches makes it tricky to properly articulate the top note – and it is often the top note that needs to stand out. Fast, swept arpeggios in rock often end with two notes on the top string, so an additional pick stroke is played.

Using strict alternate picking on these arpeggios might seem like a challenge at first, but it will pay off in the long run. Once again, look to players like Steve Morse, John Petrucci or your favourite bluegrass guitarists for inspiration, even if this isn't your normal listening as a jazz guitarist.

## Shell Voicings

Before we look at licks using drop 2 arpeggios, let's take a quick look at arpeggios based around *shell voicings*. A shell voicing contains just the root, 3rd and 7th of a chord (you might have heard them called *guide tone voicings* too). The notes can be arranged in any order, but I'm going to play them as 1, 3, 7, as this arrangement is the easiest to play on guitar and the most useful musically.

The 1, 3, 7 and 1, 7, 3 version of an Ebmaj7 shell voicing are shown below.

**Example 4e**

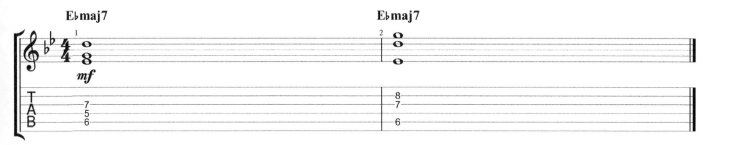

The 1, 3, 7 voicing is much easier to work with because the intervals contained inside it are smaller. There is a 3rd between 1 and 3 and a 5th between 3 and 7. As you will see later in this chapter, I often use a shell voicing arpeggio as a super-imposed structure over another chord. In other words, it's not too often I'll play a Cm7 shell voicing arpeggio over an actual Cm7 chord!

## Shell Voicing Exercises

The exercises below arrange the 1, 3, 7 shell voicings over groups of three adjacent strings. This is the easiest way to learn them and you can also easily play them as single chord voicings as well as arpeggios. Practise both on each exercise.

Since the shell voicings are arranged in three-string groups, I could have made four sets of exercises, but I rarely use the lowest three string set, so I've decided to omit it to help you focus your practice on the most useful applications of the concept. You can, of course, easily explore this yourself once you are comfortable making music with the ones below.

Again, we're in Bb Major and the first set of voicings places the lowest note on the 5th string. The lowest chord in Bb Major available on the 5th string is Cm7.

The shell voicings in this exercise are often used as chords, because the 3rd and 7th are placed on the middle strings where they work well in the musical range of the guitar. They connect extremely well with drop 3 voicings, which are probably the first jazz chords you learnt, and sound great in Bossa Nova and Samba rhythm patterns with alternating basslines.

**Example 4f**

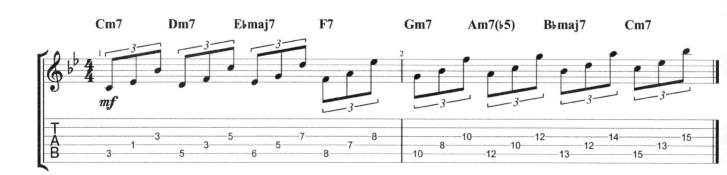

The following set of shell voicings is played on the 4th, 3rd and 2nd strings, with the root on the 4th string. The lowest available chord in Bb Major on the 4th string is F7. (Ebmaj7 would include an open string which we want to avoid right now).

**Example 4g**

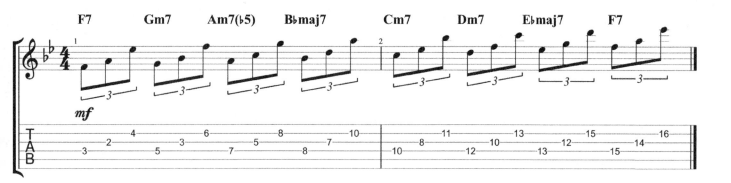

Finally, the last string set is the top three strings: G, B, E.

**Example 4h**

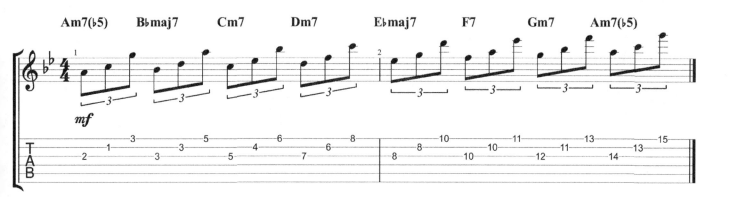

I often use shell-voicings to superimpose the 3rd, 5th, and 9th onto a different chord. For example, a Gm7 shell voicing contains the notes G, Bb, F. These can be seen as the 3rd, 5th and 9th of an Ebmaj7 chord (Eb, G, Bb, F).

| Interval from Eb | 1 | 3 | 5 | 7 | 9 |
|---|---|---|---|---|---|
| EbMaj9 | Eb | G | Bb | D | F |
| Gm7 Shell Voicing | | G | Bb | | F |

Discovering ways to connect these shell-voicings to chords you already know makes them a lot more fun, interesting and useful to learn.

One way to visualise and connect shell-voicings to drop 2 chords is to notice where they form part of a drop 2 voicing. For example, look at the first Am7b5 shell voicing in Example 4h. If you add an Eb on the D string you create a drop 2 Am7b5 (or Cm6 voicing).

The connection to drop 2 voicings hints at how I use shell voicings on this string set, but I normally play them as arpeggios.

## Shell and Drop 2 Arpeggio Examples

The examples in this chapter make use of the arpeggios on both the II and the V chords in the cadence and should give you some good ideas on how to apply these arpeggios to your own playing.

The progression is a II V I in Bb Major: Cm7 – F7 – Bbmaj7. When dealing with the F7alt I highlight the A note – which is important as it's the 3rd of F7 – but I also use the altered notes like Ab, Db etc. This does make the naming of the notes inconsistent, but at the same time makes it easier to relate to an F7alt chord and the key of Bb Major.

Example 4i begins by ascending a Cm7 drop 2 voicing with the root on the 6th string. The range of a drop 2 arpeggio is a 10th (an octave plus a third), so they're great to use if you want the dramatic effect of a melody moving from low to high very quickly.

The line continues with a quartal arpeggio built from G over the F7 chord, before the second half of the F7 line descends the arpeggio built on the 3rd (Am7b5).

C and the Eb notes nicely encircle the 3rd (D) of the Bbmaj7 chord where the line resolves.

**Example 4i**

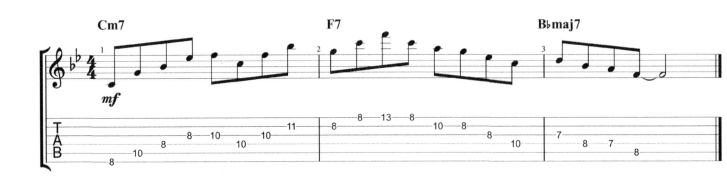

The second example uses shell voicings as super-imposed arpeggios on the Cm7. In this case the arpeggios used over the Cm7 are built on the 3rd (EbMaj7) and 5th (Gm7).

The F7 line is built around the F Altered Dominant scale and is based around the only minor pentatonic scale found in parent Gb Melodic Minor scale, Ab Minor Pentatonic. The line begins with a Gbsus4 triad and moves into a descending Ab Minor Pentatonic scale to Eb.

The Eb is resolved to the D on BbMaj7 and finishes with a D shell voicing arpeggio on the BbMaj7.

## Example 4j

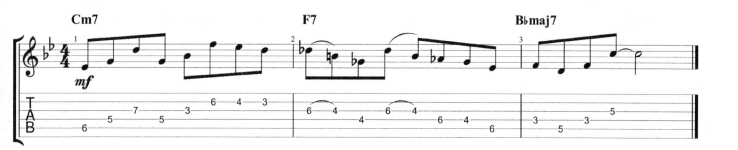

The next lick uses a Gm7 shell voicing over the Cm7, which is connected to an Ebmaj7 arpeggio. Again, this is an example of how both drop 2 and shell voicing arpeggios can move the range of the melody a long way in a short time.

Over the F7 chord, the line is again constructed from the F Altered Dominant scale, which sounds typically bebop, with a trill in the second half of the bar.

The melody resolves to the 3rd (D) of Bbmaj7 and continues with an ascending quartal arpeggio built from D.

## Example 4k

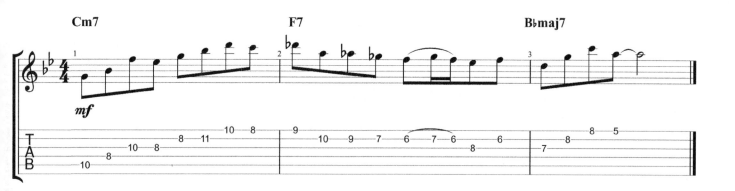

One of the most common soloing devices in jazz is to play an arpeggio built on the 3rd of the chord. In Cm7 this is an Ebmaj7 arpeggio. From the 7th (D) it continues ascending a Cm triad.

The F7 altered line starts with an Amaj7 shell voicing that contains the 3rd (A), #9 (G# / Ab) and the b13 (Db / C#). This is a handy structure to spell out a 7#9b13 sound. This is followed by a descending Gbm(maj7) arpeggio leading into the Bbmaj7.

For the Bbmaj7 chord, I play a drop 2 inversion of a Dm7 arpeggio which resolves step-wise to the high F.

## Example 4l

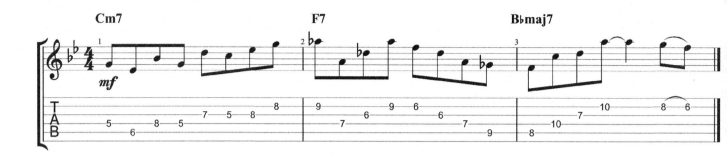

In Example 4m, the line over Cm7 begins with an Ebmaj7 shell voicing which is connected to a Gm triad via a short scale run.

I was thinking in terms of tritone substitution (B7) when I wrote the F7 part of this lick. It contains two arpeggios, first a B triad then a drop 2 Ebm7b5 arpeggio. The reason for the B triad is more obvious, but the Ebm7b5 is a common upper structure voicing of a B9 chord.

Over B7 one might play the B Lydian Dominant scale, but F Altered contains the same notes, so it's often debatable which scale you are playing. However, *thinking* B7 when writing F Altered lines can be a great way to access melodic ideas you might not otherwise think of.

## Example 4m

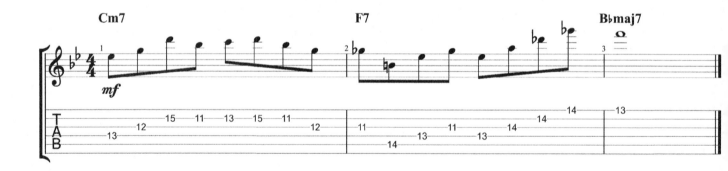

In this next example, the opening phrase is a clichéd Cm line in a 1 2 b3 5 pattern, played descending. The second half of the bar ascends an Ebmaj7 drop 2 arpeggio.

Over the F7 chord I'm thinking B7#11 (Lydian Dominant) and F7alt to construct a dominant line, but in a subtler way. The line contains a B major triad combined with an Amaj7 shell voicing. I associate the placement of the B triad on the neck with the B7 chord, but you may see it as a pure F7 Altered line.

The line resolves to the 5th (F) of Bbmaj7 and closes with a D Minor Pentatonic phrase.

**Example 4n**

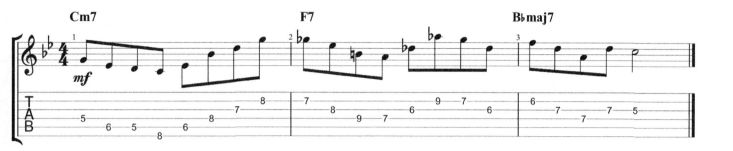

I often chain arpeggios together and in this lick I apply this idea to some drop 2 voicings.

The lick begins with an ascending Ebmaj7 arpeggio and the final two notes are used to encircle the first note in the Cm7 drop 2 arpeggio that follows to help the range of these two bars reach two octaves.

The melody played over the F7 chord is constructed by combining two descending arpeggios that counteract the ascending movement of the first bar. The first arpeggio is an Ebm7b5 played from b7 to root, followed by an Amaj7#5 descending arpeggio that resolves to the 9th (C) of the Bbmaj7.

**Example 4o**

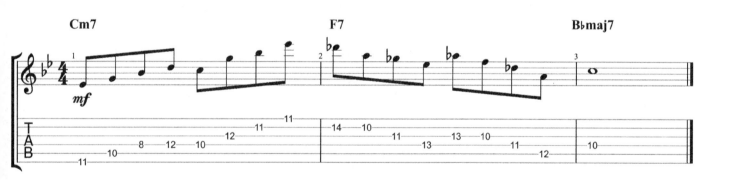

This lick is another example of cascading shell voicing arpeggios.

The shell voicings used for the Cm7 bar are built from the b3 (Ebmaj7) and 5th (Gm7). The three-note groupings of the arpeggios breaks up the natural rhythmic groupings of the even 1/8th notes that we normally feel the bar in.

The first part of the F7 line is a descending Ebm7b5 followed by a scale turn that resolves to the 3rd of Bbmaj7. The line concludes with a quartal arpeggio built on the 3rd (D) that ends on the 6th (G) of Bb.

**Example 4p**

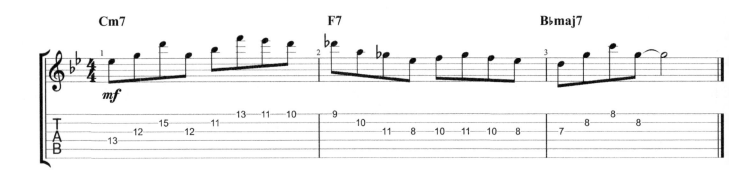

Using the root position drop 2 voicing as an opening statement lets it double as a sort of rhythmic accompaniment. Since the root of the arpeggio is low in pitch, and the notes spell out the sound of the chord, it sounds like a lower voice is laying down the harmony for the following solo melody. Bach and Paganini used a similar idea in their solo violin compositions. Kurt Rosenwinkel also takes this approach, but he tends to use triads, not drop 2 voicings.

The minor pentatonic scale also contains a few shell voicings. In this example I use Ab Minor Pentatonic over the F7alt chord and the first part of the phrase is a descending Abm7 shell voicing arpeggio. From the low Ab the melody skips up to Db and descends the scale to resolve to the 3rd (D) of the Bbmaj7.

The cadence is tagged on the Bbmaj7 with a quartal arpeggio built from D and an Fmaj triad.

**Example 4q**

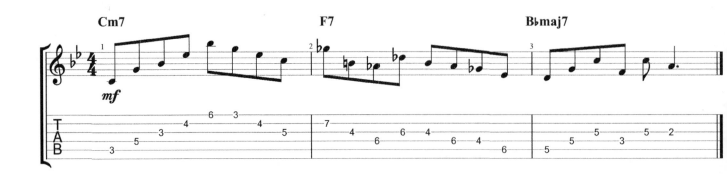

The final example of this chapter begins with a drop 2 arpeggio built on the 3rd (Ebmaj7). It descends from the top note (G) through the arpeggio built on the 5th of Cm7 (Gm7). These two arpeggios imply a Cm11 sound.

This is followed by a Gbm(maj7) arpeggio on the F7 chord. The Gbm(maj7) is played as a drop 2 arpeggio before a scale run from the high A in the arpeggio resolves to the 3rd (D) of Bbmaj7.

The D is followed with a Bbmaj7 shell voicing that ends the lick on the 7th (A) of Bb.

# Example 4r

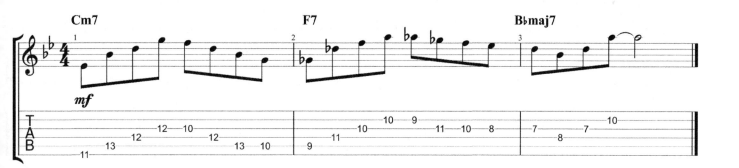

# Chapter Assignments

Here are a few ways to work on this material and expand on it to get more out of it.

- Check out shell voicings in a single scale position. This will really help you to connect the melodic ideas to its musical context, so you can easily combine it with other arpeggios.

- Write 5 licks with the arpeggio chaining concept from Example 4o where you combine a "normal" arpeggio with a drop 2 voicing.

- Check out drop 2 voicings in a single scale position. Besides the benefits mentioned above, you will also find that you really get to know what notes are where in both your drop 2 voicings and your scales. It is also a nice technical challenge to play.

- Write 5 licks with shell-voicings built from the 3rd of the chord. This is a very effective arpeggio to use both for m7 chords and altered dominants. Mike Moreno uses both in his solo on *Out of Nowhere*.

- Start practising drop 2 voicings in inversions and use those as well.

All of these exercises will increase your knowledge of the guitar neck and your ability to work with these types of structures. You will begin to dig into more ways of understanding the notes of the arpeggios against a chord and get better at emphasising specific extensions or alterations over a chord.

# Chapter Five: Exotic Jazz Scales

Another important aspect of modern jazz guitar technique is the use of "exotic" scales. In other words, scales that are not often covered by mainstream music education but can be helpful in a jazz context. There are many possible candidates to explore, but in my opinion, there are two that are extremely useful. They demonstrate some exciting points of advanced theory and, above all, make a great noise! These are the Augmented and Tritone scales. Both are *synthetic scales*, which means that they don't belong to a specific key and are constructed via a more theoretical or "mathematical" process.

In modern jazz it is now quite common to mix both tonal and atonal (synthetic) elements when writing modal music, but these ideas can also be applied when soloing on tonal chord progressions. The Diminished, Augmented and Whole Tone scales are all popular choices. First, let's examine the Augmented scale.

## The Augmented Scale

The Augmented scale is a six-note symmetrical scale constructed from two augmented triads placed a half step apart. It is a common feature in the music of modern players like Allan Holdsworth and Michael Brecker, but there are recordings of its use back in the mid-1960s by players such as Oliver Nelson and Wayne Shorter.

An easy way to think about constructing the Augmented scale is to combine C augmented (C E G#) and B augmented (B D# F##) triads. (It's obviously a lot easier to think of the F## as a G!) These two triads don't have any common notes and if you put them in order of pitch as a scale you get this:

**C D# E G Ab B C**

You'll notice that I've written the G# as an Ab to avoid having the notes G and G# next to each other in the scale.

In this chapter I refer to the enharmonic notes as either D# or Eb, or G# and Ab depending on their context, or whichever makes the melodic idea clear. Sharps and flats become a bit meaningless in atonal situations like this.

Example 5a illustrates the C and B augmented triads.

**Example 5a**

There are two ways to play the scale. One relies on its symmetrical nature and arranges it in a two notes per string pattern. It places one note from each triad per string and moves across the neck over two octaves.

The second uses a fingering more like a standard scale position and lays out the notes in one position of the neck.

Whichever way you play it, you'll notice that it is symmetrical, built from pairs of notes a semi-tone apart that are separated by a major 3rd interval.

**Example 5b**

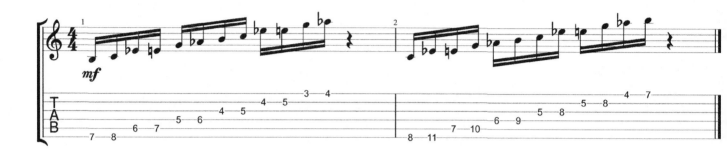

## Important arpeggios and structures in the Augmented scale

As you saw in its construction, the augmented scale is made from two triads that are both symmetrical in major thirds, so the scale itself is also symmetrical in major 3rds.

This means that once we know which triads and arpeggios are available on the first two notes of the sale, all these ideas can simply be shifted up and down in major 3rds and they will always work.

The most useful structures inside the augmented scale (in C) are:

| C Major | C | E | G | |
|---|---|---|---|---|
| C Augmented | C | E | Ab | |
| C Minor | C | Eb | G | |
| CMaj7 | C | E | G | B |
| CMaj7#5 | C | E | Ab | B |
| CmMaj7 | C | Eb | G | B |
| Cm#5Maj7 | C | Eb | Ab | B |
| B Augmented | B | Eb | G | |

There are plenty of options on the root note, C but the only really useful option on the 7th (B) is the augmented triad. The ideas in the table above can be played as chords from the 4th string in the following way.

**Example 5c**

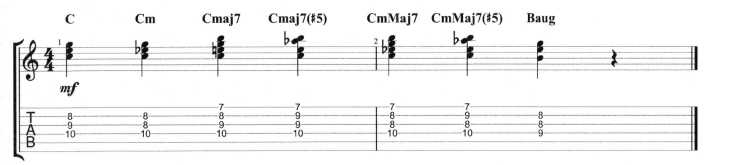

The symmetry of the scale means that any chord or arpeggio can be moved up or down in major 3rds, so in the key of C, all the C options (C major, C augmented, C minor etc.) are also available with the root notes E and Ab/G#).

The B augmented arpeggio can also be moved up and down in major 3rds and is therefore available on the notes D# and G (F##).

This unique symmetry means that arpeggio-based jazz lines can be moved up and down in major 3rds and is a big feature of how solos are constructed with the augmented scale.

## The Tritone Scale

The tritone scale is another synthetic scale like the diminished or augmented scale. It is used by many different musicians and I have heard it in music of Arch Enemy, Jimmy Herring and Michael Brecker.

The fact that the tritone scale is symmetrical makes it easier to use on the guitar in some ways, because we're already used to moving set patterns (like barre chords) in a symmetric manner.

The tritone scale is constructed from two major triads a tritone apart. Beginning on G, it is constructed from a G major triad (G, B, D) and a Db major triad (Db, F, Ab). When these notes are organised from low to high, it creates the scale:

**G Ab B Db D F**

The scale is shown below and is written it out in its most common fingering. Notice how the symmetry moves position from string to string.

**Example 5d – Tritone Scale – symmetrical fingering:**

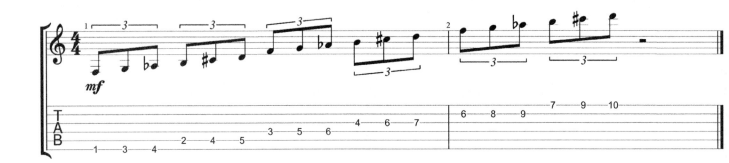

Some of the most useful chord/arpeggio structures in the tritone scale are:

| G Major Triad | G | B | D | |
|---|---|---|---|---|
| Gb5 | G | B | Db | |
| Gsus(#4) | G | Db | D | |
| G7 | G | B | D | F |
| G7b5 | G | B | Db | F |
| G7sus(#4) | G | Db | D | F |
| Bdim Triad | B | D | F | |
| Bdim | B | D | F | Ab |

Due to the tritone symmetry of the scale (two major triads played a b5 apart) all the triads with the root note of G are available on the Db note too.

The most important structures are written out below. Some of them are difficult to play as straight chords, but are shown to illustrate what is possible. You can work out your own drop 2 voicings of these chords elsewhere on the neck.

**Example 5e**

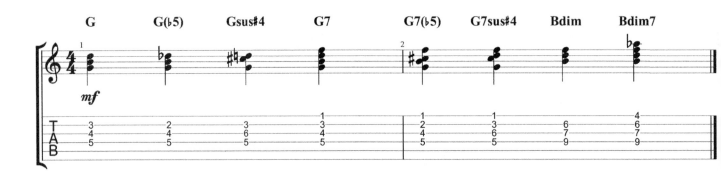

60

## Augmented Licks

The five augmented scale examples below are played over a II V I in C Major.

The Augmented scale does not have a tonal scale "sound" and is used more as a special effect in jazz. Most commonly, it is superimposed over a chord to create an unexpected sound – which is what you'll discover in the musical examples that follow. For instance, below I use the Augmented scale over Cmaj7. It grabs the listener's attention because the Cmaj7 is meant to be a point of resolution in the II V I progression – a place where the harmony stands still rather than keeps moving.

Feel free to isolate the augmented parts of the licks below and experiment with them in a more modal context. Also, bear in mind that throughout I have written the scale using the most appropriate sharps and flats for the key, so these might not always be enharmonically "correct".

The first part of the lick over Dm7 is a Dsus4 triad which is played until the G on beat 3. The remaining part is formed of a descending Dm triad.

The G7 altered line is based on an Abm(maj7) arpeggio with an added 9th.

The augmented scale line on the Cmaj7 chord is constructed from three descending Maj7#5 arpeggios: Emaj7#5 (beginning on D#), Cmaj7#5, and finally Abmaj7#5 which resolves to the 7th (B) of the Cmaj7.

The scale adds altered extensions to the Cmaj7 such as #9 and b13 which will resolve to a chord tone of Cmaj7. This means that the C Augmented scale can be used as a kind of melodic suspension of the Cmaj7.

**Example 5f**

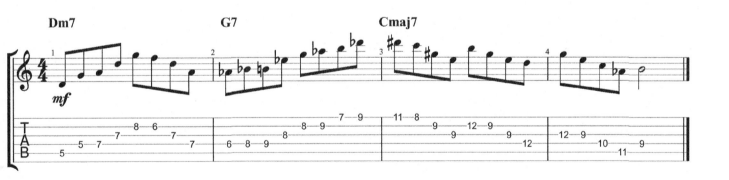

Playing arpeggios in non-sequential patterns can be a creative way of generating new melodic ideas for your solos. Example 5g begins with an Fmaj7 arpeggio over the Dm, played in the pattern 1 5 3 7. This is followed by an ascending Dm7 arpeggio.

The G7alt line is built around a Db7 arpeggio idea, which you can think of as a straight tritone substitution.

The augmented line in this example is arranged in a two notes per string pattern. This works because the augmented scale has such a distinct, angular sound it can create strong melody in its own right, not unlike superimposing a pentatonic scale.

**Example 5g**

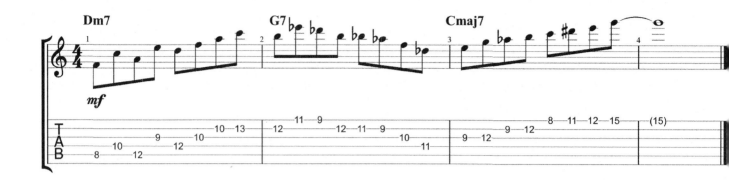

In the next example, the line played over Dm7 is a second inversion Dm triad followed by a four-note melody using a Gsus4 triad.

The sus4 triad idea continues over the G7alt chord with a descending Ebsus4 triad.

We know that triads are one of the main structures in the Augmented scale and major triads are especially useful, since they are created from augmented triads spaced in major 3rds. In this example the triads are chained together by moving backwards in major 3rds.

The E major triad is followed by a C major triad that continues into Ab major. The melody is resolved by the notes B and E, two chord tones of Cmaj7.

**Example 5h**

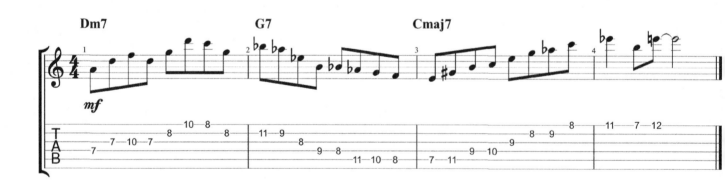

The next example features a very "guitaristic" concept. For the Dm7 part of the line, an Fmaj triad is played on one two-string set, followed by a Dsus4 triad on the next two-string set. The final two notes connect the phrase to the dominant chord and continue the upward movement.

The line over G7 is constructed from a descending Fm7b5 arpeggio that continues into an Abm(maj7) arpeggio. Both are strong arpeggios from the G Altered scale.

Besides the obvious symmetrical melodies that are often created with the augmented scale it is possible to explore a more scalic approach to writing jazz lines. Example 5i illustrates this while still working with the three major triads in the scale.

The first triad is a root position Cmaj which continues into an Abmaj triad. The final triad is a melody made with a first inversion Emaj triad. The line ends on a high E, the 3rd of Cmaj7.

**Example 5i**

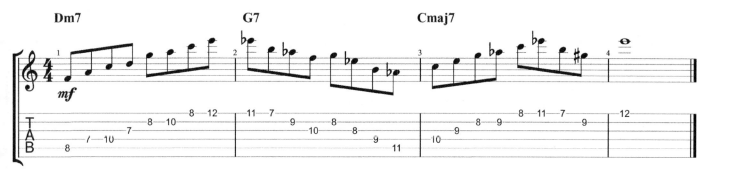

This lick next demonstrates shell voicing arpeggios on the II and I chords, a topic covered in detail in the previous chapter.

The first part of the Dm7 line is formed from an Fmaj7 shell-voicing which moves into a Dsus4 triad. Notice how these two ideas nicely break up the movement of the melody and stop the line from running in just one direction.

Quartal harmony and pentatonic scales can create similar-sounding melodies and both sound more "modern jazz" than "bebop". Over the G7alt chord the melody uses Bb minor pentatonic which is the only minor pentatonic scale in the G altered scale. The melody is simple but doesn't need to be complex as the pentatonic scale is a strong structure in itself.

For the Cmaj7 chord the line relies on the symmetry of the scale and is constructed from maj7 shell-voicings in the Augmented scale. These are Emaj7 moving to Abmaj7 and finally Cmaj7.

The concept of shifting structures forms a big part of the sound of the Augmented scale in jazz. In this example, the idea is of shifting upper-structure sounds over the underlying Cmaj7. The symmetry helps make melodies that sound strong and logical to our ears. It is normally important to take care to resolve these sounds to a chord tone of Cmaj7.

**Example 5j**

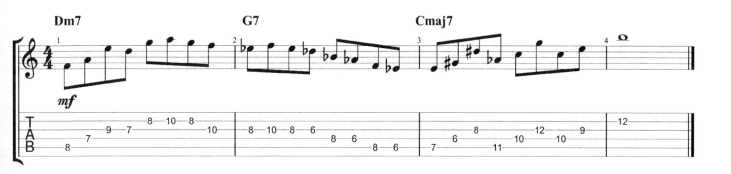

## Tritone Scale Lines

While the Augmented scale is applicable to several chord types, the tritone scale is a dominant scale and will only work for dominant and diminished chords. The examples in this section therefore apply the tritone scale to the V chord in the II V I chord progression.

The line over Dm7 line is formed from a simple scale run and descending Dm7 arpeggio.

For the G7 chord, I alternate between Dbmaj and Gmaj major triads. Notice that the 3rd and 5th of the Dbmaj triad encircles the root of the Gmaj triad.

The Cmaj7 line is formed from an Esus4 followed by a Gsus4 triad.

**Example 5k**

A spread triad is created when one note is shifted an octave. In Example 5l, a D minor root position triad (D F A), has its F dropped an octave, so when played ascending the notes occur in the order F D A. It's like a drop2 version of a triad (see the chapter on intervallic structures for more information).

Spread triads are a fantastic way to add large intervals into jazz lines. The Dm7 line in this example opens with a first inversion Dm "spread" triad. From there the line continues with a descending A Minor Pentatonic scale run.

One of the structures built on the root of the tritone scale a Majb5 triad. The G7 line begins with a Gmajb5 triad played from the 3rd (B). The second half of the line is a Dbmaj triad.

The transition to the Cmaj7 is a resolution from the b7 of G7 (F) to the 3rd of Cmaj7 (E). The line continues with an E7sus4 arpeggio in root position. Over Cmaj7, E7sus4 contains the intervals 3 (E), 13 (A), 7 (B), and 9(D). It's a great arpeggio to spell out the Cmaj7 sound with some choice extensions.

**Example 5l**

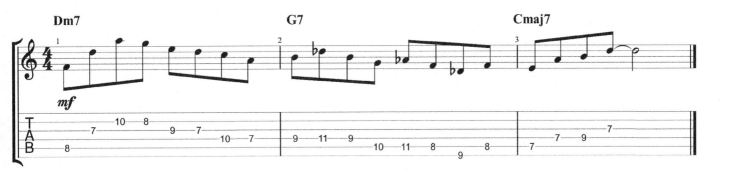

Using the D Minor Pentatonic scale is an easy way to access other sounds over a Dm7 chord. It seems obvious, but the fact that the scale has a different structure and contains larger intervals makes it useful for creating less stepwise melodies.

Symmetrical scales can be played with symmetrical or repeating fingerings, making them useful for creating purely visual or pattern-based ideas. But this can also lead to a solo sounding predictable and boring, so should be used with caution.

The scale pattern used on the first three beats in this example uses this idea combined with the top part of Example 5d. The final note of the scale run becomes the highest note in a first inversion Db major triad which resolves to the 3rd of Cmaj7.

A Cmaj7 shell-voicing arpeggio pattern is used on the tonic chord in the final bar.

**Example 5m**

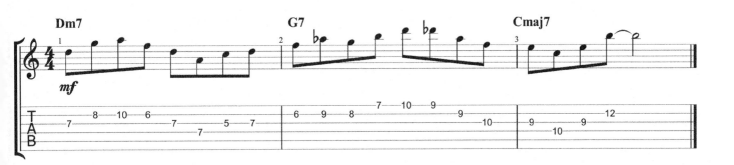

Creating new symmetrical fingerings is an important step when taking advantage of the symmetrical aspect of the tritone scale. This example demonstrates this concept and expands on the previous example.

The first part of the Dm7 line is a Dm9 arpeggio followed by an A Minor Pentatonic scale run. You will often hear Wes Montgomery use maj7(9) and m9 arpeggios in his solos.

For the G7 chord, a three-note pattern is built from the 1 (G), b9 (Ab) and 3 (B) which is moved up a tritone on the next string to repeat from Db. The final note in the pattern is again used as the first note in the following (Bdim) triad which resolves down to the 6th (A) of Cmaj7.

**Example 5n**

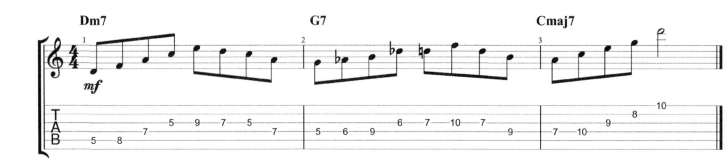

The final example begins with a four-note chromatic enclosure targeting the root of the Dm7. This is followed by an ascending Dm7 arpeggio. The enclosure suspends the sound of the chord until beat 3.

Over G7 is another example of how to chain G and Db major triads. The triads are played with one note per string and are linked more freely with different patterns played on each one. This approach takes advantage of the symmetry, but also explores more creative ways of making melodies.

The Db triad resolves to the 5th (G) of Cmaj7, and the melody is tagged with a descending quartal arpeggio from D down to E.

**Example 5o**

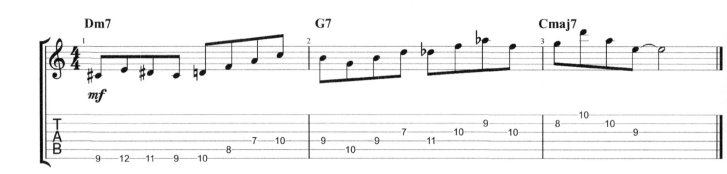

# Chapter Assignments

Write a set of 5 or more licks over a progression, or a short solo over a song, using:

- The C Augmented scale on a Cmaj7 chord using the three triads

- Lines that include triads but are not symmetrical

- Lines that use the Augmented scale sound more than the arpeggios found in it

- The two triads from the tritone scale

- The symmetrical scale patterns of the Tritone scale (as shown in Example 5d)


There are, of course, many ways to explore these exotic scale sounds and it's a good idea to focus on using them as a set of shifting sounds on top of a chord, as well as scalic ideas in their own right.

In the case of the Augmented scale, the first "shifting" characteristic to explore is the augmented triad built on the root (C, E, G# in the key of C). In the tritone scale that is the b5 relationship between the Gmaj and Dbmaj triads. Most soloists use these sounds to slide in and out of the tonality on top of a chord. It's a big part of modern jazz vocabulary, so start here and don't feel you need to reinvent the wheel. There's a lot to explore and the most commonly used approaches work very well.

To use hear the Augmented scale and its melodic fragments used more scalically, listen to Allan Holdsworth on *The Devil Takes The Hindmost*. This illustrates this concept well, even if the patterns are a bit stretchy!

# Put it in a Blues!

This book has covered a wide range of topics and ideas that you can use in your own improvisations. It will take time and patience to assimilate these into your playing.

To demonstrate how you might apply some of them, I have written a Bb Blues solo. This will hopefully give you a longer, more realistic demonstration of their application over a common chord progression.

Analyse the following solo and look out for the different concepts used in the lines (something you should do every time you transcribe a solo). I've included a short analysis of this solo, but try to analyse the transcription yourself before reading it! That way you can see if you missed anything, or whether we have different interpretations of a phrase. There is always more than one way to interpret what's going on, so even if you hear something else it may be correct.

Since this is a real solo and not just a combination of everything in this book glued together, I won't analyse every single phrase. Instead, I focus on those parts that illustrate a topic covered in the book.

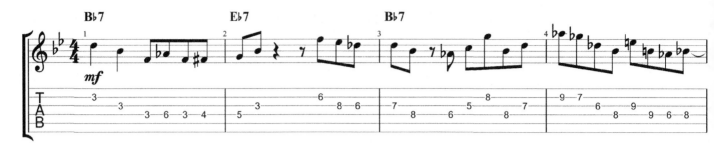

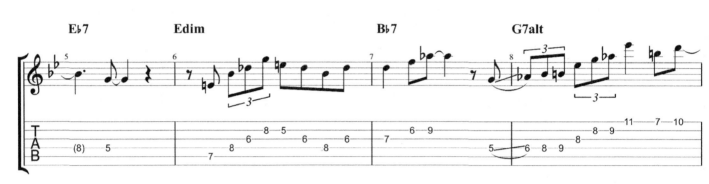

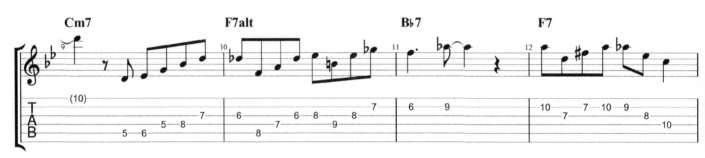

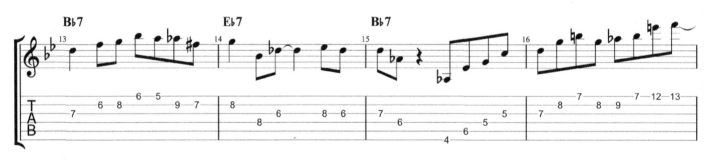

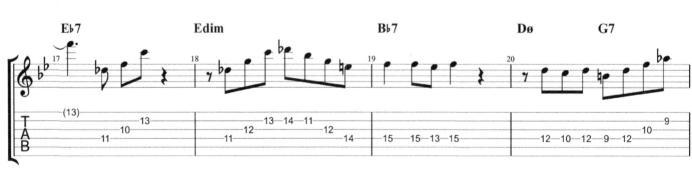

# Analysis of the Solo

## Chorus One

Bars 1-2: Chromatic enclosure targeting the G on beat 1 of the Eb7 bar

Bars 3-4: The line moving from Bb7 to Eb7 first uses the diatonic shell voicings Abmaj7 and Bb7, then transitions into a Bb7 altered lick using an E and F#(or Gb) triad pair.

Bar 6: The Edim triplet arpeggio on beat "1&" is a drop 2 voicing.

Bar 8: The G7 line is an altered line based on an Abm(maj7) arpeggio.

Bar 10: The F7alt line uses the triad pair of Aaug and Bmaj played with different patterns. Don't get stuck playing long predictable lines using a systematic approach.

Bar 12: The F7 line uses Dmaj and Abmaj triads from the diminished scale which create a F7(13b9b5) sound over the F7 chord.

## Chorus Two

Bar 13: A chromatic enclosure from beat 3 targets the G on Eb7.

Bars 15-16: The line moving to the Eb7 arpeggio starts in bar 15 with a low drop 2 voicing of Abmaj7. You can interpret this as Fm7 or as an arpeggio on the b7 of the Bb dominant. Bar 16 is a triad-based line using the diminished scale triads of Gmaj and Emaj that resolves to the 9th on Eb7.

Bar 17: A Dbmaj7 shell voicing is used over the Eb7.

Bar 18: This is a quartal arpeggio built from Db over the Edim chord, similar to the top part of an Edim(b6) drop 3 voicing or an Eb7(13) drop 3 voicing. The quartal arpeggio transitions into an Edim arpeggio that resolves back to F on the Bb7.

Bars 19-20: The Motif of bar 19 is continued throughout this chorus with added phrases and variations. The first variation is on the Dm7b5 and transitions into Bdim arpeggio on the G7. This is typical when using the C Harmonic Minor scale on the G7.

Bar 21: The Cm7 line uses two three-note quartal arpeggios built from C and F that end on beat 1 of F7.

Bar 22: The line on the F7alt chains together a first inversion Ebm7b5 arpeggio and an Amaj7#5 arpeggio.

Bars 23-24: The motif returns in a developed form first on Bb7 and then on the F7alt.

## Chorus Three

Bars 25-26: The motif begins on the top of the form and concludes in bar 26.

Bars 27-28: The three major triads Bb, D and Gb demonstrate one way to use the Augmented scale on a blues. Notice that the scale doesn't fit with the chord but is used as a special effect until it's resolved.

Bars 29-30: There is a motif stated on Eb7 and then developed on Edim.

Bar 32: A B quartal arpeggio creates a G7#9 "Hendrix" sound on the G7alt chord. The 1/8th note triplet pattern incorporates some larger intervals into a line.

Bar 34: The line on the F7 uses a tritone substitution and adds the IIm7 chord before the tritone substitution to outline an F#m7 – B7 line. This uses an Amaj7 arpeggio then a first inversion Ebm7b5 arpeggio.

Bar 36: The F7 line is (again) the quartal arpeggio from the 3rd to create a Hendrixy F7(#9) voicing.

Bar 37: The line is resolved to the E, which is the b5 of a Bb7b5.

# Conclusion

Throughout this book we have explored some of the more advanced modern jazz concepts used by guitarists such as Kurt Rosenwinkel, Adam Rogers and Mike Moreno, and saxophonist Michael Brecker. Concepts such as the effective use of triad pairs for soloing, for instance, is now an essential part of the modern jazz vocabulary.

I have endeavoured to give you the appropriate tools to develop these ideas and absorb them into your own playing. More than that, I hope I have inspired you to explore, experiment and take these concepts to places you may not have thought of without some provocation!

Remember, there is no single "correct" way to approach these ideas. You must feel free to adapt, change and combine them according to your musical tastes and what appeals to your ears. That way, they will become a natural, organic part of your musical language.

Learn jazz – make music!

*Jens*

Printed in Great Britain
by Amazon